Praise for
You Are a Supermom

You Are a Supermom, part memoir, part myth buster, is a refreshing read about shedding the layers of perfection. Gina's vulnerability addresses the pressures parents face and the road bumps we all experience in life and parenthood. She weaves real-life solutions on the power of standing in your truth, bursting through patterns, and broadening your perspective through self-reflection and grace into every aspect of her writing.

Tahverlee

Social Impact Entrepreneur and Founder

moontempleschool.com

While "Moms Do it All" is a common myth that needs to be busted, you can learn balance; and, ironically, accomplish more when you are healthy, harmonious, and happy. If you are exhausted, burned out, and wondering how you'll get through the next few years (until that magical time when our kids grow up to be independent, successful adults), then you need to read this book. You will learn how to give yourself some grace and not try to "do it all," and you'll see exactly why it's so imperative that you learn how to put yourself first.

Gina's vulnerability and willingness to share her struggles is so refreshing. While reading the book, I felt like I was sitting with a dear friend who was baring her soul in a way that only friends can. I now see that by allowing myself to prioritize my own health, spirit, and passions as much as those of my family, I am modeling a healthy way of living in abundance and happiness instead of lack and sacrifice.

Marta Spirk

Mom to Triplets, Empowerment Coach & Marketing Strategist

martaspirk.com

In this powerful parenting book, Gina Fontaine is raw, real, and relatable, sharing strategies and stories most moms would try to keep hidden for generations. There is no pretension here, and the ways she offers you a look at your role as a parent through good times and through hardships will give you insights you'll use for years to come.

Elle Ingalls

High Performance Coach

elleingalls.com

Gina Fontaine is a dedicated and passionate mother, and an inspiration to mothers everywhere. Her book, *You Are a Supermom,* is about her own adventure of discovering parenting to be the greatest challenge of her life while feeling as if this was her greatest weakness. She eventually transformed it into her greatest strength. She began to author her own life to help others do the same; and now supports mothers by helping them recognize the super strengths they already have.

In her raw transparency, naked truth and while bearing her burdens to become greater blessings, she has found a way to inspire and motivate. Gina shines her light and guides you out of the darkness into the light to be the Supermom you already are.

Thank you, Gina on behalf of mothers everywhere!

Cynthia Gardner O'Neill

Ultimate Wellness Living

Rapid Recovery Coach

ultimatewellnessliving.com

This book is a must read for parents in our fast paced world. Gina Fontaine's honest reflections will help you pause and reflect to find inner peace that will enhance your parenting skills and creative thinking. My family is raised, but this will help me be a better grandparent. Love this book!

Kathy Berg

YOU ARE A SUPERMOM

YOU ARE A SUPERMOM

5 Ways to Reclaim Your Superpower and Thrive as a Mom

BY

GINA FONTAINE

QUANTUM SHIFT
PUBLISHING

Books may be purchased in bulk by contacting the publisher or author at:
Support@QuantumShiftMedia.com

ISBN: 978-1-955533-00-3 (Paperback)
ISBN: 978-1-955533-04-1 (Ebook)
Library of Congress Control Number: 2021912093

QUANTUM SHIFT
P U B L I S H I N G

Quantum Shift Media
Denver, Colorado
www.quantumshiftmedia.com

Editing, book design, and cover design by Quantum Shift Media

Printed in the United States of America

Dedication

This book is dedicated to Miles who has taught me how to be a Supermom. And to my mother, Sharon, the original Supermom.

Table of Contents

Introduction

I am a woman who understands and accepts her fullness.

I have experienced the bliss of the birth of my three children, the horror of witnessing my former husband abuse our oldest child, and the trauma of parental alienation during the early days of my divorce. I come from a Midwestern family of 10 children. I am the youngest. I rose to the top of everything I did as a kid. Straight As. Best athlete. I aspired to be the greatest, and I saw huge success in my future. When I found myself on welfare with a defiant child who was in and out of juvenile detention and dropped out of school after my divorce, I wondered where I went wrong.

I embrace the good, the bad, and the ugly of my life experiences, and I still stand proud to tell my story. That is what it is to live in fullness. This book is filled with authentic, true-life stories. Many of them are jarring. My hope is that by reading about how I learned to live each day in appreciation for the life lesson being offered, you will be inspired to rise above the challenges you face as a mother. You never have to hide in shame or fear of being judged. We have stigmatized the Supermom to be a woman who sacrifices all her dreams and desires to help her kids become the best of everything.

The truth is, Mom, when your kids see YOU living your dreams, they will be inspired to do the same.

I gave birth to all three children while living in a tiny 900-square-foot Victorian home in a predominantly Black and Hispanic neighborhood near downtown Denver, Colorado. My then-husband used to worry because I insisted on running in our neighborhood with our small children in the stroller amidst the police sirens and regular discoveries of used drug paraphernalia.

We moved in 2012 from our inner-city Denver home to the suburbs in search of a more family-friendly environment. We gave our best effort to fit in as minorities in an up-and-coming community. However, I lost my pioneering spirit when my oldest son, then 8 years old, came home from school with strangle marks on his neck.

The school had called to forewarn me that he had been in an altercation with another student. Later, I found out that one of the kids had pinned my son down by the neck during group activity time. The teacher didn't catch it right away. Apparently, that young boy had witnessed gang violence in a park just days before.

The guilt I felt when I found out that my son had been an innocent victim of violence was immeasurable. How could I be so naïve to think my kid could fit into a school where he was part of the 2% minority Caucasian population in this inner-city school?

I was committed to my neighborhood school. I was not going to be one of those parents who choiced their kids into the schools in the more affluent parts of Denver. My heart was in it to build community connections.

But seeing strangle marks on my son's neck, my heart was broken.

"We have to leave Denver!" I practically commanded my then-husband. "Miles isn't safe in this school."

Within months, we put our house on the market, sold it in two days, and transferred our oldest to the Littleton suburban school district. There, he would swim in a sea of vanilla sameness. *At least I won't have to worry about my kid's safety anymore,* I told myself.

The irony was that the site of the worst school shooting in history stood just two miles from our home.

Before I moved from Denver, I remember talking with one of my city girlfriends.

"I hear suburban moms all have big butts from sitting all day playing carpool captain," she told me.

I laughed and said, "That can't possibly be true. That is so unfair to say."

I would come to find out that moms in the 'burbs are much less inclined to exercise than their urban counterparts.

I can now reflect on my suburban life in the trenches. I used to try to do it all to keep up with the status quo. Then my life unraveled seemingly thread by thread until one day, I realized there was nothing holding it together any longer.

Now, in 2021, I have moved back to the city. I observe walking school buses (a group of kids walking to school with one or more adults) and moms running with strollers in central Denver's busy Washington Park. The parks and streets in the suburbs were not bustling with this much activity. Are most of the moms in the 'burbs spending hours in their minivans carting kids around or commuting long hours to work?

As Supermoms around the globe became grounded during the pandemic, many of us took time to reevaluate what is truly important in life.

I love that my kids can be content entertaining themselves without structure or organized activity. You might find my youngest, Ian, age 10, stacking foam rollers and jousting them with a broomstick. Or he might set up 10 cups in the living room and play bowling. My daughter, Vienna (13), is prone to baking outbursts that often land happily in our bellies. And these days, my oldest, Miles (17), has taken an interest in fringe politics and avant garde media outlets.

The years of trying to be a traditional, stressed-out Supermom as defined by my social conditioning wore me down and eventually broke me, my marriage, and my family.

Sometimes you have to let go of everything to be whole again.

Today, I can look back on my life in the traditional Supermom role and say she was a crazed, moody bitch. As a yoga teacher and fitness professional, I wanted to lead by example. Yet, as a perfectionist, I felt like a farce going from the calm enlightenment of my restorative yoga class to the clamor of my strained home life living with an alcoholic partner.

As long as I could make everything look perfect, I thought, *everything would be okay.* Turns out that living your life under false pretenses is exhausting.

I admit that my inability to stop, be still, and relax contributed to the demise of my marriage.

Now, as a woman who has walked through the fiery hells of a contentious divorce and endured the sometimes-violent backlash from her three kids, I have learned to surrender being everything to everyone.

That process has been messy, and, to a recovering perfectionist, I have agonized at seeing my whole world go up in flames.

The last time my ex left our home, he scornfully shouted at me, "The Holocaust begins now. You are going to burn!"

I am the phoenix rising from the ashes of her former stressed out Supermom persona. I am emerging now as an empowered Supermom.

My life took many twists and turns during the tumultuous final years of my marriage and then the divorce. After failing time and again to live up to my self-imposed expectations, I finally came to realize that I had to give up this mythical life I was trying to live.

Mom, I see you hiding in the shadows of your social media posts. It really is okay if you skip posting your kids' Halloween, Easter, and first day of school photos.

When I became an empowered mom, I finally heard my kids say, "Mom, would you ask us before posting photos of us on Facebook?"

I had never thought of it when they were toddlers and preschoolers. But, of course, they are people, too, and I must respect their right to privacy. Now I ask my kids' permission before posting photos of them to social media. My oldest son has advocated the most for his right to privacy. When I began insisting on checking his cell phone, he adamantly refused and imposed a lock screen to ensure I would stop meddling. These days, with apps that allow us as parents to see our kids' every move and communication, society tells us that being a responsible parent means keeping tabs on your child's every cell phone interaction.

Does this really build trust? I know there are predators out there and our kids are at risk, but I do believe that danger is way overblown. These days, from my empowered mom stance, I am more prone to trust that I have instilled values in my children that enable them to screen their own online interactions. And, as you will read, my kids wandered into some dangerous territory during their independent explorations.

Throughout this book, I will share stories of how I have stumbled and fallen and gotten back up again trying to be the best mom possible. By being frank, I hope to remove the stigma attached to serious issues like teenage suicide attempts, juvenile delinquency, high school dropouts, and other risky behaviors youth engage in.

When I became a single mom in 2017, I had to change my lifestyle. Taking care of myself had to rise to the top of the list of priorities. My former spouse may never change. His insults and abusive actions may continue, and that is why I must stand in my truth like never before. A wise older gentleman I met on a hiking trail just days after my divorce advised me, "Every day, look at yourself in the mirror and say, 'I love you.' I guarantee that your ex may even behave worse through the years, but you have to be strong for your kids."

I thought that once my divorce was finalized, I could go on my merry way and start my new life. In truth, it has taken every bit of the four years I have spent trying new ways of parenting, dating guys who had no interest in relationships while I tried to convince them I would make their life a fantasy, and exploring different ways of running my business. In the end, what I found to be the secret to my success on the road to becoming an enlightened nurturer and empowered woman, was the disposal of five myths that no longer served me.

In this book, I will share stories of failure and triumph. The process of change is rarely a straight one, and I hope that I can help you shorten your own journey of self-discovery, Mom, so that you, too, can realize the fulfilled and loving woman you are. You might say, "I love my kids with all my heart, Gina. They are everything to me."

To that, I say, "Wonderful!" But…, can you say the same to yourself?

Try it. Say, "I love myself with all my heart. I am the center of my own Universe."

My former spouse relentlessly drilled into my kids' heads, "Your mom is selfish. She doesn't really care about you." When I stopped listening to him and realized that by putting myself first I could be a better mom, I started to live life with a soul purpose. I will share with you the steps I took to get there by dispelling each of the five myths, chapter by chapter.

The first myth, "Good Moms Always Put Their Kids' Needs First," was the first to go. Self-care is all the buzz these days, but what does that really mean anyway? When I ask women what types of self-care practices they engage in, I hear things like, "I take a bubble bath" or "I treat myself to a manicure once a month." Is this really caring for your soul, or is it an external manifestation of a desire to really love yourself?

I am not knocking bubble baths and manicures, but I am suggesting that loving yourself goes much deeper than purchasing fancy personal-care products and services. We will explore the concept of receiving in this chapter. Most women give to the point of exhaustion and rarely take dedicated time to nurture themselves. This model of caregiving can lead to unhealthy levels of stress that will age you quicker. I will present the case for moms to take more quality time for themselves so that they can give from a place of fullness. The first step is figuring out what activities and tasks are depleting your energy.

I recently saw a meme that said, "Motherhood: Powered by love. Fueled by coffee. Sustained by wine." That perfectly described me. Because we live by Myth #2, "Moms Are Master Multitaskers," we must keep a steady stream of caffeine in our bloodstream to keep ourselves sharp and on task. This line of thinking is flawed because caffeine and other substances we use to boost productivity actually create calamities in our bodies. You will learn about the compounding effects of stress on your body in this chapter, and I will make the case for reducing your duties as an important part of longevity and health. Out of a state of chaos, we find ourselves engaging in activities that have no purpose or any relevance to our soul purpose or desired way of being. I will discuss the concept of discovering your deeper intention and how to connect with yourself daily to create inspired actions that align with your soul purpose.

Your greatest superpower in any situation is peace. We hear Myth #3, "Being a Mom Is Tough," all the time, especially during 2020 when we juggled so much at home while in quarantine. Here is what I have come to understand. I am who I perceive myself to be. In this chapter, we will explore the idea of mindset and shifting your sense of who you are.

I have had plenty of practice being stressed out and over-whelmed. Now, I tend to ask myself this question, "Will this decision bring me peace?" Sure, I still act on impulse and sometimes yell at my kids. But throwing hissy fits daily has taken a backseat because peace is driving my reality now.

As a Type A, competitive, driven woman, the concept of slowing down sounded good to me but it always eluded me because I was too busy. I will share how my life has moved from anxiety to tranquility using the power of the pause and being with my emotions, whatever they may be, instead of pushing them away by filling my schedule full of activities. My sense of self-worth no longer comes from filling my schedule. I know that I am enough, and you are too.

When you are enough simply as you are, you will stop over-scheduling yourself and your kids. As you begin to slow down and enjoy the moment, Myth #4, "Being a Mom Is Exhausting," will be replaced with "being a mom is exciting." I spent years blaming myself for my oldest son's less-than-conventional path. You will read many stories about how I struggled to get control of my defiant teenager. Once I stopped trying to fix, heal, and change him, and turned the focus on filling myself with love, he began to make better choices. No amount of force or punishment will ever change your kids' behavior. Our kids want to be heard and respected. Asking questions and seeking out learning opportunities for deep connection are two skills I have acquired, and I will share them with you in this chapter.

When your kids look back on their youth as an adult, do you want them to remember you as the mom who (a) kept the house clean, cooked meals, drove the kids to practice, and served on the PTA board; or (b) made playdough and sculpted animals with them and had snowball fights in the backyard?

I would bet you chose (b). When my daughter entered kindergarten, I took on a full-time administrative job, which required more than 40 hours per week to get the job done. I still cleaned the house, grocery shopped, served on the school committee, and somehow survived to tell the story.

Within a year, I realized I could not do it all. I had gained 10 pounds, and I had used every one of my paid sick days. At the time, my mother, Sharon, who raised 10 children, said to me, "Gina, I don't know how you do it all."

I replied, "Mom! You raised 10 children. I only have three."

"Yes," she agreed, "but I never worked outside the home. You are tough as nails, honey."

Once I quit my job and took on a part-time job and began to pursue my own business dreams, I felt more fulfilled. That was also the time I hired a business coach. Making the payments for that service stretched me. And as I expanded myself, the mundane daily tasks fell lower on the list of things to do, and I found myself saying "no" to obligations that did not serve my higher purpose.

I quashed Myth #5, "Mom Does It All," when I decided to stand in my truth and only say "yes" to those events and activities that feel aligned and purposeful to me. Practicing mindfulness and being in my own body help me discern what is best for me and my family. In this chapter, I will teach you the techniques I have used to successfully lighten my load.

Chapter One

Myth #1: Good Moms Always Put Their Kids' Needs First

Myth-buster: Most moms believe that being a mother requires them to put their children's needs and desires first.

Reality: You can be an even better mom by taking care of yourself first. Here is something to keep in mind: always putting your children first will age you quicker.

I attended a networking meeting with a group of 25 women entrepreneurs. The topic for discussion was fear and how it limits us. As we introduced ourselves, each woman spoke aloud one of her biggest fears.

The first woman, who wore fancy high heels, said she owned a custom shoe business. She stood and said, "My biggest fear is that I will not see my kids through to adulthood."

Yet another mom with short hair rose and told the group, "I just don't have the energy I used to. I had kids later in life and now, as a mom of teens in my 50s, I am afraid I won't have the energy to be a fun grandmother."

And then the very next woman stated the same fear.

The pattern I saw was alarming to me. Are moms really afraid they will not live to see their kids to adulthood? How could this be?

My kids run out of the kitchen when I start dancing to '80s' hits while I cook, and they beg for mercy when we go out for hikes. They wonder how they will keep up with me! I want every mother to experience the fullness of her radiant self. Mama, you are a beautiful shining goddess! And you deserve to shine that light in the biggest way.

I know you may not feel that way when you have poop on one hand and spit-up running down your back. Or when you must pick your teenage kid up from the school detention center after his third minor offense.

Through both of those experiences, one thing has always remained a constant: I have exercised in some way, shape, or form every single day.

As a 46-year-old woman who has gone through the fiery hells of divorce and who is now restructuring a household as a single adult, I have definitely experienced time constraints and energy demands that have brought me to my knees.

I endured even as my kids defied me in the early days of my divorce, literally throwing shoes at me in their rebellion. Could it be that they were only reflecting my own internal chaotic state?

I steadfastly maintained my routine of walking, running, yoga, and hiking even when I might come home to find the house in shambles from the three kids (then ages 14, 9, and 7) taking full advantage of mom's absence.

Peace and harmony in the household is an inside job. You have got to get right with yourself, Mom, if you want your home to lend itself to spontaneous bouts of celebration and spark.

So, why do we give up most of the things we love to be a good mom?

I asked myself this very question as I noticed how many of my interests and pursuits (such as drumming, dancing, tennis, and long hikes) had fallen away since I had become a mother. And I was very unhappy.

After the birth of my third child, I was diagnosed with post-partum depression. Undoubtedly, there was a hormone imbalance, but more significantly, my life was way out of balance. I was juggling two kids at home from school in the summer with a newborn. At the time, my husband's mother was terminally ill. Understandably, his attention was focused mostly on her.

At first, I resisted taking medication, but when angry outbursts and irritability became my new normal, I knew something had to change. I took the medication.

But I soon discovered the side effects were not worth it. I had no sex drive; I was restless; I gained weight, and my emotions were flat. I quickly said, "No, thank you!" I continued to rage with unresolved hormone imbalance in hopes that this stage would pass.

At the time, I exercised daily, teaching fitness classes and training private clients. Sure, I was active, but I wasn't filling myself up. I operated from a depleted energy supply most of the time. My thyroid was whacked, and my emotions were out of control.

In autumn 2016, I was in the midst of launching my signature holistic wellness program for expectant moms called Power of Pregnancy. I had run three instructor training sessions, and one of the largest school districts in Colorado signed a contract with me to offer the program to its pregnant staff members.

My business had money in the bank, and I invested it right back into myself. First, I purchased an electromagnetic device that increases circulation and, thus, vitality. Having already sold three of the devices, I knew I was making a sound investment that at this writing has paid my family back more than five times its worth. My former spouse disagreed, but I knew I was making a good decision for the whole family in the long run.

Secondly, I hired David, a business coach. And in that first one-on-one session, he asked me the question that would change my life forever: "What is the number one thing holding you back from success in your business?"

I blurted out, "My marriage." Then I recoiled and said, "What did I just say?"

David assured me that was a great place to start. It didn't necessarily mean I had to end the marriage to succeed in business. And yet, four months later, I ended up filing for divorce.

My former spouse allowed me the time and space I needed to launch my business, but as I began to succeed and become healthier and happier, he didn't share in my accomplishment. On the contrary, he seemed envious.

Let me be clear, I am not saying, moms, that if you are unhappy and unfulfilled in your marriage that it's over.

Relationships are divine mirrors. They reflect exactly where we are on our growth journeys. My partner and I could not find common ground, try though we did. He would argue that I gave up on our relationship too soon. I found that I was making conscientious efforts to be more of myself. That only intimidated him and made him feel less worthy. He said it was my duty as a wife to pull him out of the pit of despair he had fallen into after the death of his mother.

In his mind, I was cold, heartless, and unfeeling for not picking him up in the dull, down moments. Instead of celebrating my success, it felt like he tried to sabotage it.

Now, four years later I can look back and see that things may have ended differently if we had both recognized the balance of the Yin and Yang -- the feminine and the masculine, the give and receive, the fill-up and empty.

Instead, it became a tally sheet of *I did this for you, so now you do this for me.*

A relationship founded on balance sheets is doomed to fail.

When two people who are secure and in love with themselves join, there is a healthy exchange of energy that naturally lifts the relationship to a higher level. Admittedly, I did not love myself when my marriage ended. Loving myself was not even a concept I had explored.

As a parent of three children who tried to do everything perfectly, I had nothing to truly give myself. I didn't even know that I had no inner awareness of what I truly wanted. I was just running from one activity to the next. Even my exercise was for others. I rarely spent time by myself.

Now, I love spending time alone. I am my own best friend, and that allows me to be a better mom, friend, lover, and daughter.

Receive the Gift of Love

Sometimes parenting sucks. There, I said it -- and I would bet that you have had that thought, too, especially on those days when you are working from home and the kids are running rambunctiously or ignoring your pleas to go outside and play. When your attention is scattered or you are worried, frustrated or angry do you feel fully energized? Moms struggled through the days of remote learning during the global pandemic playing teacher, disciplinarian, and household manager, and many women were trying to work from home at the same time. It's no wonder we moms (and dads) felt frazzled after a year of this. Many of us felt so exhausted we had no capacity to reboot at the end of each day.

I am a big proponent of bragging about, celebrating, and owning your success. Most women are too busy *doing* to slow down enough to celebrate their successes. Girls are trained from an incredibly young age to marginalize their successes. At school, I can remember purposely holding back the right answers because I did not want to be labeled the *smart one*. There was far more glory being labeled the jock. As women, we suck at receiving compliments, and we are even worse at asking for help.

Does this scenario sound familiar to any of you?

"Sherry, I love those new pants. They look great on you."

"Yeah but my butt is still huge and I need to lose weight," Sherry laments to her friend.

Instead of turning the compliment into a negative, imagine how it would have felt if her reply had simply been, "Thank you."

To graciously receive a gift is one of the greatest gifts we can give the gift giver.

Doesn't it feel awful when you offer a compliment to someone and they shrug it off as untrue? Be a gracious receiver and you will give from a place of fullness.

What do I mean by fullness? The Bible references fullness as surrendering totally to the divine i.e., let go and let God. You are a sovereign being when you let go of your ideas of how it should be and instead stand fully in the truth of how it is for you right now even when it looks messy.

What if instead of blaming and shaming yourself for losing your temper with your children, you recognized that you are running on empty. In that moment of losing control, what could you do to regain composure? Pray? Go outside? Sit in the bathroom with the door shut and breathe deeply? It is ok to own your imperfections. Your children do not trigger you or cause you to lose control. The anger and frustration were already there and until you own it, accept it and nurture the place in you that is wounded, you will continue to spout off.

You are the Divine. Perhaps you were brought up believing that God is an entity outside yourself. The radical concept of living in your fullness starts with recognizing that God planted a seed in you to become a unique expression in the world.

I believe that God is inside me *and* outside me. The Divine lives in me and therefore all I need is inside myself. I do not need to look elsewhere. Like an acorn, everything I need is already there. The potential to grow resides in my ability to tap inward and feel the energy and wisdom that is always there and that usually happens when I slow down. From that place of deep knowing, I can then ask for help and that is when I must go into elevating my awareness, noticing signals all around me.

Guidance can show up in line at the grocery store and during a walk at the park. When I am living my life aware and open to receive messages from divine guidance, I begin to realize that I don't have to walk this journey alone. One of the many gifts from being in quarantine was the removal of so many of the daily distractions.

I also encountered my deepest, darkest self; those places in me that I have been running and hiding from and denying were even there. I realized that I was making my pain and fear wrong. By the looks of social media, everyone else was living such glorious lives. One mom was posting her weight loss success while another was happily posting her daily color-coded organized schedule for her kids, Let's get real. We all have shadows and it is okay to acknowledge that part of yourself, too.

Pain and fear are not bad or wrong. Comparison will crush your spirit and deplete your energy faster than anything. I still cast judgment on myself even after years of consciously stating that I am enough and that everything is here to help me.

After 4 years of living in survival mode, I finally have the capacity to implement more order and structure at home. I have been on a deep dive into the darkest caverns of fear and loathing of myself. My outlet for discomfort is movement. I feel through movement. I release anger and frustration through movement. And one way I do this is by playing a vigorous game of tennis. I can become very vocal and swear like a sailor on the tennis court.

Recently, I was playing tennis and I wasn't playing my best. My body was exhausted after moving into another home and then taking the family on a week-long vacation. I ignored my body's signals to rest because I needed to move and vent my emotion. I tore a ligament in my knee that day and now I will spend the next 6 months getting surgery and recovering.

Being in fullness means accepting what is. I had just purchased a new tennis racket and I had signed up to play in leagues for the first time in 9 years. I was finally reclaiming one of my greatest joys. And now I am struck down with an injury. What a cruel joke. Or is it a gift?

Spiritual teacher, Matt Kahn, says the mark of a truly enlightened soul is someone who can say in all situations, "Yes! Just like this."

The first step toward living in fullness is feeling gratitude. Have you ever said, *Thank you God for showing me my weakness so that I may continue to grow?* Feeling appreciation for even the challenges can be the most difficult step on the path of spiritual growth. Matt Kahn also says, "Everything is here to help you."

I think of how Jesus willingly sacrificed his life in the most horrific way. He prayed the night before his crucifixion, "O My Father, if it is possible, let this cup pass from Me; nevertheless, not as I will but as you will" (Matthew 26:39).

When I began the journey of my divorce, I realized that it was going to be long and arduous. If someone had shown me a movie reel of what I would have to go through four years ago, I never would have followed through with the divorce. I expected that my kids would understand that our life would be better without the daily arguments between mom and dad. I expected that my former spouse would realize that we were no longer growing together and accept that ending our marriage was in the best interest of everyone.

That is not how it turned out at all. Could it have been any other way? Would I have learned what it truly means to surrender my will to the divine order if the path had been easy?

What I have discovered is that in accepting the messiness of the process and discovering that I am not a victim, I now feel worthy to receive everything my heart desires. Perhaps living in fullness is taking full responsibility for your life and the outcomes and then making the necessary changes to create a life that is guided by your Higher mind, that inner knowing that you cannot get it wrong when you listen to yourself.

Be Yin Your Feminine: The Art of Receiving

I began to look at being a woman very differently when I learned that the feminine (Yin) archetype in the Taoist Yin and Yang philosophy was actually the receiver -- the cup to be filled, the sunset to the sunrise.

I see women as goddesses, an ideal to be honored and venerated. Instead, most women put themselves down and put others' needs before their own. Aren't women supposed to give selflessly, you might ask? But at what cost? What a perspective shift it was for me to begin thinking about filling myself up, first, so that I could be more present and joyous for my family.

Then I began to think of my own mother and how when I was a young school-age child, she was the last one out of bed. My older siblings helped me make my lunch and get ready for school. By her 10th child, my mother earned the right to sleep in as long as she wanted. She was modeling for me then how to place my own needs first, and yet, I would have to go through my own journey of feeling exhausted and depleted to discover that for myself.

Could it be that when women show up happy, fulfilled, and joyous, they better support the male innate desire to give?

I wrote a presentation entitled, "Yin and the Feminine Art of Receiving." I offered the first one as part of my church's women's retreat in October 2018, a year after my divorce.

A year earlier, the pastor at our church (who asked me to be the keynote presenter at the retreat) had been instrumental in helping me discern whether divorce was the right choice. My former spouse and I went to her for counseling immediately after I filed for divorce. She suggested that we live in separate homes for up to a year and have monthly date nights to check in and connect. Since my spouse's family lived locally, she advised that he move out with a family member during this period of separation. My former spouse refused to move out, saying that the home was his and he wouldn't give it up. At that point, Pastor Laura said, "You two are not only not on the same page. You aren't even in the same book. I don't see any reason to stay together, and I don't make that recommendation very often."

With that, we left and continued to live in the same home for another week until my former spouse left one evening saying, "Have a nice life." He then went to a hotel and attempted to take his life. His mental instability rendered him unable to co-parent for a period of time. The courts granted him six hours per week with the kids, and I was drowning trying to keep myself and the family afloat.

Pastor Laura became a mentor during the months leading up to my divorce. She prayed with me and assured me that love and light always win. I remember her telling me that this period of time was my Good Friday and that one day my Easter would come.

When she invited me to be the keynote presenter at the annual women's retreat, I was honored. Yet, I felt like my life was in shambles. How could I possibly have anything of value to share with these women? I decided to accept her gift. I had spent the entire year being Yin and Yang -- mom and dad -- doing it all, being all things for everyone. I would go days without sleeping, working a 5:30 a.m. to 12:00 p.m. shift at a gym and then stepping full force into mom, business owner, and household manager mode for the rest of the day.

When my former spouse refused to help me with house payments and, after his suicide attempt, he proved to be unstable and unable to co-parent effectively, I became the sole provider for my kids. Lest I fall into the trap of blaming, suffice it to say, I decided to take my life back slowly, bit by bit. In all honesty, that did not happen until I humbled myself enough to receive the outpouring of help and words of encouragement from my friends and supporters.

I could have pushed all the support away, saying, *I can do it myself!* but that would have been foolish and quite honestly a slap in the face of God, who blessed us with such abundant grace.

On Easter that year, I didn't know how I would even provide Easter baskets for my kids. When I expressed this concern to a longtime client, she and her husband sent me a generous check, saying, "You have given so much to us through the years, and this is a small expression of our gratitude. Give your kids the best Easter." With that generous offering, I was able to not only gift my kids with a fun Easter but also buy them necessities, like clothing.

Another example of generosity I received came from the staff at the elementary school my kids attended. The teachers and administration saw my daily struggles firsthand. I didn't have the money to pay for field trips and things that I could have easily covered in the past. The school found a way to help me. One day, the principal called me and said, "When you pick up the kids today, can you please stop by the office to pick up something?" The school secretary handed me a manilla envelope filled with gift cards to restaurants and cash offerings. "The teachers and staff understand you are going through a tough time, and they volunteered to pool their resources to help you out," she told me. "You have given so much to the school community with the garden and your service on the school accountability committee. This is our way of giving back to you."

There were many other examples of generosity that I received. I found a jar of calming tea in my mailbox with a kind note one day. Friends brought meals over. One day, a complete stranger came over with a trunkful of bulk-sized food to stock my freezer. She said, "My friend forwarded your email asking for assistance, and I just wanted to help. It must be challenging to feed three kids and keep up with all the housing costs on your own." She unloaded the food, and I never saw her again. Surely, she was an angel.

In my learning to receive and then sharing that experience at the women's retreat, I began my own transition to becoming a willing and open beneficiary of gifts. Some women cried as I shared my story. I realized that the concept of serving yourself first is not clearly stated in the Christian teachings.

I ended my presentation with a quote from a former client who lived to be 101. He called it the 11th Commandment. "Honor thyself. In the end, there is only you and you have to take care of yourself."

I celebrate you, Mom, for being authentic, beautiful, and aligned with Spirit just as you are. In your most depleted moments, I know it sucks. Are you putting off taking dance lessons or joining a softball league because your child's activities precede your own desire to grow and advance yourself? What if your child watched you at one of your events or practices? Do you think that would leave a lasting positive impression on them? I went to my mother's activities long before I began to join organized events. My mother unknowingly instilled in me the value of self-care by modeling it through her lifestyle.

The number of women dying prematurely of stress-related illnesses is on the rise. Could this be due to the increasing amount of responsibilities that women are taking on? It is no longer enough to run a household. Now, full-time working moms are expected to do it all, and with less free time available, women are giving, physically to the point of making themselves sick. Authorities such as the Centers for Disease Control and the Mayo Clinic estimate that the stress response accounts for as much as 90% to 95% of disease.

Are we, as women, out of balance in terms of the Yin and Yang? Yang is the masculine energy of doing and giving. I would surmise that women, as a whole, need to allow more time and space to get back to their Yin (receiving) essence so that the Yang (the more active aspect of life) becomes more fulfilling.

Stress itself is not a bad thing. It is our reaction to pressure and the body's physiological response to unmanaged stress that wreaks havoc. When I was working full-time and had paid sick days for the first time in my career, I used every single one of those sick days. I had never been an ill person before. Why was my immune system seemingly compromised? I would theorize that I was depleted and exhausted to the point where even exercise was draining me. Working, keeping up with the household, keeping up with the kids' activities, and trying to maintain a marriage was too much output. I quit that job after one year because I could see my health declining.

How many women do you know with autoimmune disorders, thyroid diseases, or breast cancer?

If we were taking time to pause and honor the need for rest (Yin), could we possibly prevent disease conditions from developing? When we pause, we can hear that quiet voice telling us what is truly important for tending to the highest good of all. We really must prioritize our health and well-being and put an end to the sacrificial mother archetype. We have all heard the analogy of putting on your own oxygen mask in the airplane before putting on your child's mask. The point is, if you have nothing to give, then you will not be able to serve your child's needs at all.

You are a beautiful goddess, mom. And when you shamelessly step into that reverent role, everyone around you will step in to help and appreciate you even more. Value yourself, and others will respect you even more.

Own Your Value

Stop negating yourself today. You are enough, and all the extra things you do really need to support your wellness. If they do not, then ditch them and begin practicing daily gratitude in place of daily repentance.

What do I mean by that? I grew up Catholic, and the guilt thread runs heavily through my ancestry. You may know the thought process: *I fell short, so now I have to punish myself or do something to make things better.*

One of my biggest lessons has been that my children's behavior and choices are not a direct reflection of who I am or an indicator of poor parenting skills. When my son began cutting classes sophomore year, I would ask myself, "Where did I go wrong?" I ruthlessly bashed myself for his unruly behavior. And as my self-worth plummeted, my son continued to make choices that would harm him and our family.

I blamed myself for the decisions Miles was making. Even though he would blame me for calling the cops and increasing his anxiety, at the end of the day, he had to be accountable to himself for the choices he was making. He would say things like, "I have to smoke weed to stay calm because you are always making me feel so stressed out." I felt bad that I could not seem to create a loving, supportive home environment for my son. At one point, he went to live with his Dad for a year and a half.

During that time, I was able to start the process of forgiving myself and celebrating the positive role I had been playing in my son's life. Every therapist and counselor I spoke with during those dark days would commend me for never giving up on Miles. It turned out that the greatest gift I could give Miles towards promoting his self-worth was to acknowledge that I was doing the best I could with the resources I had.

Now, instead of feeling like I always have to make up for everything, I now embrace compassion, acceptance, and tolerance. Even though I lose my temper less often now with my teenage son, I accept that I will slip and get angry and say things I don't mean. I accept the anger, now, rather than push it away. The expression of it is less erratic when I choose to slow down and receive my emotions as energy in motion. It is not bad to feel rage, sadness, or fear. I have found that when I negate these emotions and label them as bad, that is when I lose my cool. And then that starts a cycle of feeling bad because I fell short once again. I recognize that negating myself only weakens my spirit and disconnects me from my soul purpose.

Finding Your Soul's Purpose

In order to reach your potential, you need to discover your soul's purpose. It is that driving force that keeps you moving forward. It is deeper than your life purpose. Each soul is here to fulfill a different mission while in this physical body. You discover it by recognizing what excites you. Where do you get so lit up that you lose all sense of time and space? What is your unique contribution to the world? Knowing your soul's purpose is a process of self-discovery and acceptance.

I learned about this in 2015, when I took a four-day workshop where each participant explored within and discovered his or her unique soul purposes.

After days of self-reflection and asking myself challenging questions, I, with the guidance of the facilitator, created the statement: *My soul's purpose is to connect with Spirit and live in strength.*

Now does that say anything about my position or goals in the world? Not at all. It does provide a framework for how I live. Each and every day I find ways to connect with Spirit. I might dance, meditate, play my drum or choose an angel card or walk in nature to get out of my head and into my heart. As a child, I got perfect grades, I was an intellectual and while that may have gotten me through school with accolades, it was not until I discovered what lights me up that I could blend my intellect with my joy.

When I created my "soul purpose" statement, I almost wish I had not created the intention to "live in strength." The Universe has a much more rigorous training program for building personal fortitude than any gym-based strength training I have ever done.

On May 13, 2020, I received a phone call from the hospital that my son had put a gun to his head and, fortunately, failed at a game of Russian roulette. Every ounce of strength I had been gaining was brutally tested that day. When the nurse shared the news with me, my knees collapsed and I sank to the ground. I screamed. I went to the basement and threw yoga bolsters against the wall. I called a family member who added insult to injury saying, "You know he is only trying to get your attention."

I had a friend staying with me at the time and she witnessed my 30-minute rage that turned into spirited laughter and gratitude that my son was alive. She could not believe how strong I was to face such grave emotions. I felt every ounce of them. I expressed them and processed them in that moment. The past few years had prepared me to face that difficult situation without blaming myself or sinking into despair.

Thanks to my prior struggles, I have endured the global pandemic with relative ease. No doubt, it is difficult to face the base-level challenges of loss of safety, security, and support due to the challenges presented by dealing with the global pandemic, but as my 10 year old wrote on my birthday card in 2021, "you pushed through 2020 like it was nothing."

I Am Safe, Secure, Supported, Valued, and Loved

I used to walk the 1.5-mile loop by my house reciting this mantra: *I am safe, secure, supported, valued, and loved.* With little money to provide for my kids and even less moral and emotional support, I had to tell myself that it was all going to be okay. I felt like a farce convincing myself of the truth of this mantra. And yet I completely felt the Universe reaching out to support me in ways I never could have imagined.

Allow yourself to GROW,
get big and expand.
The Universe will fill the
space in ways you never planned.

My coach, David, had given me metaphors to shift my way of being. In the beginning, I was the Fiery Volcano. I was compressed and stressed and spouted off with no warning. I tended to burn everything down in my path due to the limiting beliefs I unknowingly imposed upon myself.

The new way was The Open Field. One of my assignments was to get outside daily and step into an open field to broaden my perspective.

I came to understand that, like harmony, abundance is an inside job. Thoughts create things. They form a framework for expectation and those expectations influence our language and ultimately the choices we make. If I expect abundance, then I will begin to notice the abundance of trees and birds and smiling faces. Those experiences that bring me joy will connect me to the possibility of attracting even more abundance in the form of perhaps, relationships or money. This principle is based on the Law of Attraction, which tells us that our thoughts and feelings powerfully shape our life experiences.

When I left my husband, I also lost the steady source of his income. I had little income for three months, while I waited for the court to mandate child support. The generosity of friends, family, and supporters at every turn humbled me. I felt shame for accepting public assistance and food-bank donations, but in looking back, I am grateful I had that help.

How could I, Gina Fontaine -- the high-achieving, Father Sahm award-winning, Best Female Student Athlete at Immaculate Heart Of Mary School who graduated second in her class from high school and then gained acceptance into Boston University's five-year bachelor's/master's degree physical therapy program -- end up in this poverty?

Friends advised me that I had to get out of lack and scarcity and step into an abundance mindset.

The gratitude journals and affirmations and daily walks in the open field helped validate that my life was blessed. Each day I began to write or recite what I was grateful for. I even gave thanks for my bills because those bills paid for our home and basic needs. I affirmed that everything was okay and that everything is always working out for me. Most days I would step into the open field overlooking Harriman Lake with the view of Red Rocks in the distance and I would be instantly transported from my problems. In that field, I cultivated the feeling of being open and expansive. My life problems did not disappear with these practices, but I began to realize the bounty in my life. The base-level fear of losing my home or not having enough to feed my family still existed. I felt shame for accepting government assistance. I worried about being perceived as a freeloader working the system.

I soon recognized that the assistance and support from friends and family and even the government was my abundance. My feeling of scarcity shifted into gratitude and I began to attract healthier relationships because I was grateful and full in my heart and mind.

The financial struggles would continue for years even though I was focusing on abundance and wealth. I did "money mindset" workshops and listened to "attract money" meditations but still I lived near the poverty line. Why couldn't I just get my shit together and go out and succeed?

I reread the words that my coach, David, wrote four years ago, "How would the mindset of The Open Field allow you to grow a valuable business and charge the fees you deserve?"

At the time, it seemed brash to charge $4,000 for a six-month package to work with me. To this day, I am still met with resistance because, of course, anyone can hire a personal trainer for $60 to $75 a session. What I began to realize is that when I am working for that wage (minus the 40% to 50% the club deducted), I am exhausted. I could not deliver my best service because I was more concerned about making sure I was consistently booking 20 to 25 sessions a week.

In The Open Field mindset, I love every client I work with. My clients value our time together and commit to it 100%. I realize that putting my needs first and setting clear boundaries around what I will and will not do is critical to my success. I still need to work on setting boundaries between work and family time. I am learning now that I can even weave the two together.

My kids are great now about understanding that I work for myself, and that lends a lot of freedom in our lives. They encourage my success and remind me of my goals and even help me stick to them. My youngest son enjoyed holding me accountable when I committed to writing 2,000 words a day. Each day he would check in with me, "How many words did you write today, Mom?"

My daughter has assisted me with workshops and my oldest has supported me throughout the writing of this book, encouraging me to share this story to be of service to others. It was Miles who suggested, "Mom, you need to just find that one thing that lights you up and run with it!" With that, I could let go of extraneous responsibilities and sources of income. I no longer listen to webinars through dinner time as I did in the past. I no longer accept clients I am not thrilled to work with. I find myself still wondering if I am missing out by not making daily social media posts or creating Facebook live videos. I realize that all that work had a time and place and now I can reap the abundance from that effort.

The Fiery Volcano version of me can get things done quickly and efficiently, but she also has an eruptive temper and reacts rather than responds to life. She is stuck in worry and fear. As I walk more frequently in The Open Field, I am enjoying my life and expanding my thinking and allowing rather than forcing things to happen. The trick is to not worry in those periods of waiting.

Do Not Worry

The Bible tells us not to worry. Here's a passage from the Book of Matthew, Chapter 6:

> *25 Therefore I tell you, do not worry about your life, what you will eat or drink; or about your body, what you will wear. Is not life more than food, and the body more than clothes? 26 Look at the birds of the air; they do not sow or reap or store away in barns, and yet your heavenly Father feeds them. Are you not much more valuable than they? 27 Can any one of you by worrying add a single hour to your life?*

Now I just look for the next step to appear on the path of life. Much like the birds in the passage above I am just looking for that next signal knowing that each step is pointing me in a direction towards fulfilling my soul purpose. My soul purpose guides me and with awareness, faith, and trust, I create ease in my life just by knowing that I only have to know the next step.

The Trap of Worry

Perhaps worry motivates us as moms to put our kids' needs before our own. That worry has its roots in comparison or keeping up with the Joneses.

For example, a mom (let's call her Susie) worries that her son will not live up to his potential. She hires the best tutor and pays exorbitant fees for her son to play club sports. Meanwhile, Susie and her family go into massive debt financially and energetically to ensure her son's success.

At the age of 37, Susie receives the prediabetes diagnosis. She takes the daily medication and continues with her frenzied life as PTA president, soccer mom, and business owner only to find herself in the hospital months later with low red-blood-cell count. What will it take to get Susie to put herself first? Hopefully she won't be like the 55-year-old woman whose obituary read, *She was a master multitasker. She juggled hockey practices, school board, and other extracurriculars.*

How sad. The prematurely dead mother put her kids' needs before her own, falling prey to Myth #1. I'll bet she never had a chance to hold one of her grandchildren.

What if doing less for your kids translated to being more for them in the long run? I grew up the youngest of 10 kids. My mother carted me around to *her* activities of choice. On Tuesdays, we went to a bowling league, and on Wednesdays and Fridays, we went to tennis. The bridge ladies would come over for lunch on Thursdays. I never felt cheated. In fact, I think I learned more by observing. More importantly, my mother was happy and fulfilled. When it came time to come to my sporting events, she was full of energy and pep as she stood in the stands cheering me on.

Has worry ever been your motivating factor to start exercising?

Jill, a mom I worked with, is a good example of the relationship between worry and exercise. Jill has struggled with her weight since giving birth to her infant son. She worried that she would never return to her pre-pregnancy weight. She enrolled in a CrossFit® gym and does kick-ass workouts three days a week. After three miserable weeks of enduring soreness and exhaustion, the scale showed the same number. *What was going on?* she wondered!

My theory is that fear and worry -- rather than a desire to become even healthier -- motivated Jill's exercise routine. Added to that was the sleep deprivation of being a new mom and the anxiety that naturally comes with the initiation into motherhood.

It is no wonder her body retained the weight. A body that is trapped in a chronic state of stress will not function optimally. The body's sympathetic nervous system is triggered when we are stressed. This sends out a flood of hormones that shuts down digestion, memory, and the ability to process and learn new information amongst many other deleterious physical and mental symptoms.

Jill was frustrated because she felt she was doing the right thing. But was she really honoring her body in its current condition as a recovering postpartum mom? No. She was pushing herself and in her exhausted state, those workouts were counterproductive.

That is the frustrating loop of the trap of worry. When we do anything out of fear, lack, or scarcity, we often trap ourselves into a loop of exhaustion, depletion, and desperation.

When you come from a place of well-being, your body can metabolize, digest, and function even better. When your motivation is grounded in love and care for yourself, you enter your daily practice with anticipation rather than obligation or even dread.

Be the Center of Your Own Universe

It's alright to put your own needs before the needs of others. I mean, of course, you have to tend to your baby's diaper blowout before you shower and put on makeup. I had plenty of days where I was at the club training a client and wondered midday, "Did I brush my hair today?"

Acknowledge that life will be a bit crazy for a while during that first year of your baby's life. Cut yourself lots of slack and know that your main job during this time is to be present to your own needs so that you can be more present to your baby. You don't have to climb mountains or leap giant buildings. When I was a young mom, I forced myself to run and walk even when my body probably needed recovery. People commented on how quickly I bounced back after having babies and that positively reinforced this behavior. But had I taken the time to rejuvenate, would I have been better able to handle life's bumps in the road? I was too busy performing superhuman feats to enjoy base level joys like being at home with my family.

As a culture, we place way too much pressure on new moms to recover fast and get on with life. After having a baby, I was most assuredly right there at the starting line ready to sprint even before I got my doctor's clearance to exercise. And I paid dearly, with uncomfortable conditions like mastitis, exercise incontinence, and chronic low back pain. I was terrified that I would lose my physique and not be a model personal trainer for my clients.

What if I had taken my mother's advice and just let the house get messy and rested when the baby napped? I might have felt even better physically and mentally, but all I could see was that I had way too much to do to slow down. At the time, I had no concept of yin and yang, or balancing my energy.

In many cultures around the world, new moms are left to rest in bed for the first month while family and community tend to the household tasks. In Mexico, this period of time is called *cuarenta*, a 40 day rest period with family. In Japan, women move back home for a 3 week period of seclusion after giving birth. When the body is at rest and a mom focuses her energy on herself and her baby during this adoring time, the weight comes off naturally. Many American moms don't want to undergo the inconvenience of breastfeeding. In reality, this is nature's way of passing the body fat Mom gained onto the baby who needs it.

It took going through three pregnancies for me to understand the value of slowing down. Now I say, "Slowing down is the new fitness," especially where moms are concerned.

Many moms wear the busy badge of honor. It's as if saying *I am busy* is a status symbol of success. When we are busy, we feel needed. Being needed makes us feel important. Being busy is a dangerous measure of success because the long term result is often burnout and disappointment.

What if true success is finding peace within and operating from a platform of equanimity rather than chaos?

This week, my 12-year-old daughter painted her room all by herself. She required no assistance from me, nor did she ask for it. In fact, when I offered my input, she quickly asked me to stop.

Many years ago, my mother offered me this piece of parenting advice: "When your child falls, don't immediately run to pick them up." At the time, I thought her words were harsh. But now I understand they had a deeper meaning. I realize that all the coddling and attachment-style parenting I bought into did not serve my children well. And worse, I was left feeling resentful as a depleted and empty parent.

When I had my first child in 2003, I was fully invested in the idea of being the best mom possible. I subscribed to Dr. William Sears' attachment parenting method. He encourages parents to enhance the bond with their children by wearing them in baby carriers and taking them everywhere. He also encourages sleeping in the same bed as your baby. This directly contradicts Dr. Richard Ferber's "Cry It Out Method" that so many of us were raised with.

My purpose is not to dictate which method is right for you. For me, at the time, I just knew I didn't want to listen to my tiny baby cry himself to sleep. I tried "Ferberizing" my son, and I lasted only a few nights before my soft mommy heart came to rescue my tiny, beet-red, screaming infant from the terror of being alone. I quickly ditched that method and continued to co-sleep with my son until the age of 3.

In the meantime, I tried all kinds of other methods of sleep training. There was BabyWise and Lull a Baby and the Baby Whisperer and the Stand on Your Head and Tap Your Nose Methods of sleep training. (Well, okay, I made up the last one.) But trying all these methods felt like doing acrobatics.

Seventeen years later, as I look in the rearview mirror, I wonder: *If I had known how to calm my own anxiety, would my son have slept better and learned to quiet himself?* I absolutely believe that. Furthermore, if I had been calmer I would have been better able to endure the inevitable crying as he adjusted to being alone.

My relatives said that I coddled my firstborn. I heard the criticism being whispered behind my back at family gatherings. "She does everything but wipe his butt for him," I would hear my son's aunt say long after he was out of diapers.

Disciplining my son as a toddler was extraordinarily difficult. This kid thought *time-out* was a game of hide-and-seek. I scoured the parenting books and methods trying to find the right way to parent my unruly toddler. I can't say I ever found a method that stuck, and as I write this, I am having this cathartic realization that:

> *If I had spent as much energy taking care of myself as I did reading books and attending classes in those early days of motherhood, I may have saved myself from countless hours of crying and feeling like I was losing my mind.*

I used to embody the traditional Supermom image, always there to pick up the pieces and ensure that the family system was running smoothly. Then, in 2017, when I got divorced the whole machine broke down. I thought I was doing the best thing for my family. Continuing to raise my family in a home with daily discord and arguing seemed harmful in the long term. For many years we tried to work it out with counseling. But the night my husband literally threw me out of our home, I decided in an instant that my marriage was over.

My kids were in disarray. The first was prone to violence. The second had daily screaming tantrums while the third innocently watched it all happen. For a while, my full-time job was getting each of us to counseling, and filling out motions and court documents for the divorce for which I would ultimately represent myself.

Bumpily Ever After

I am letting my children fall now. One spills paint on the bathroom floor while another periodically sits in a detention center.

I am a Supermom because I am a real Mom. I don't aspire to send my kids to the best colleges or put them on the best athletic teams.

When we were staying home more with our kids, due to the precautions we were taking to stay healthy amid a global pandemic, we were faced with the reality that *home* begins with ourselves. The heart of a happy home starts with a mother's heart. The saying, *If Mama ain't happy, no one is happy* carries a lot of truth.

I thrive even though my circumstances are challenging. I trust that my children will find their way as I tend to my own needs and offer myself grace. As I become happier and more grounded, my kids stabilize, too.

I am a Supermom. I am a daughter, a sister, a friend, a wonderful, flawed, authentic woman, a seeker of peace, a voracious learner, and a passionate lover of life.

As mothers, we have bought into some very outdated beliefs about what it means to be a good mom. Especially in these times, when many moms are balancing work, mothering, household management, and maintaining relationships, it is impossible to juggle it all.

Chapter Two

Myth #2: Moms Are Master Multitaskers

Myth-buster: Multitasking is a self-defeating fallacy. Become masterfully mindful and watch your life flow.

Reality: The brain cannot focus on more than one complex task at a time. You are more productive when you focus on one task at a time.

I used to be a self-proclaimed master multitasker. When I was fitness director for a city recreation department, I had an inordinate amount of responsibility. Among other things, I ran programs at two recreation facilities, was responsible for fitness equipment worth millions of dollars, managed a staff of 50 instructors and five personal trainers, and organized a citywide weight-loss challenge.

It was not uncommon for me to have my instructor payroll work on one desk and a marketing campaign for an upcoming event on another desk that also had a list of top-priority calls to make for that day. If an instructor called in sick, I abruptly switched gears and taught a fitness class.

I prided myself on my master multitasking and improvisation abilities. However, at the time (2014), I was starting to see research that indicated that multitasking was, in fact, impossible for the brain to do.

I dismissed that research as one-sided. I had been successful, and I had attributed my success to my mad juggling skills. How would I ever get anything done if I stopped doing it all?

Meanwhile, I had been a yoga practitioner for 20 years and still could not manage to sit still for more than five minutes of meditation. There was just too much to do. I laugh as I write that because I now realize that the way I currently operate is:

The less I do, the more I am. The more I am, the faster I grow.

Our time on earth is limited, and I don't want to clutter mine up with stuff like keeping a perfectly tidy home or checking my kids' messages on their cell phones.

As I mentioned earlier, one of my goals while working with my coach, David, was to stop being a perfectionist. The Universe provided lots of strength training in this area during the next three years while I went through a divorce, restructured my life as a single mom, and birthed a new business.

After my divorce, I went from weekly sweeping and mopping of all the floors to just sweeping visible areas and saying *good enough.*

I used to mop the bathroom floor at least once every two weeks. LOL. Recently, I had the gratifying experience of removing dust bunnies from behind the toilet because it had been six months since I had given the floor a good cleaning.

Mowing the lawn? No longer a weekly task. Not watering the lawn is a good way to save time, I discovered. It turns out brown lawns don't need to be mowed as much, and that is okay for the backyard.

Cleaning doors and baseboards? Nope. That's a task I now hand off to the kids.

I mentioned to my kids it would be healing to sort through my cluttered garage. They stopped waiting for me and finally cleaned the garage themselves to create a hangout spot.

You don't need to be fixed, healed, or changed. You only need to be loved, accepted, and embraced!

I spent much of my career in fitness trying to correct and fix bodies. In some cases, that worked. I have come to realize that being a Corrective Exercise Specialist (for which I have two certifications) implies that there is something wrong that needs to be fixed.

In behavioral psychology, there is no clear winner when it comes to reward vs. avoidance methods of altering habits. Different people respond differently. For example, my oldest son has little interest in rewards, but my youngest is highly motivated by winning a prize. I am also very reward-focused, but that is not the case for everyone.

Slow Down

Remember Myth #1, *Good Moms Always Put Their Kids' Needs First?* When you are constantly serving others, there is no time to slow down and take care of yourself.

Having a full schedule can feel like success, but the truth is, being preoccupied robs you of the experience of inner exploration. Letting go of busyness takes courage. I believe many moms find satisfaction from having many irons in the fire. With each check off the list of things to do, you gain self-worth and feel accomplished.

When you start putting your own needs first, Mom, you will begin to feel whole, healthy, and complete. The task list becomes shorter because you no longer need the instant gratification of getting it done. Life gets very chaotic when you focus only on external circumstances and other people's needs. When you are calm on the inside, you see things through a lens of peace, and life becomes easier.

But how do you slow the hustle?

5 Steps to Slowing Down

1. Start your day with prayer or gratitude and acknowledge at least 10 ways you are thankful. Stop checking your phone first thing in the morning.

2. Continue to lie still. Ask for guidance on the 3 Big Tasks that you will complete today, no matter what. Make them meaningful and attainable.

3. Ask yourself the outcome you desire for each task. How would you like to feel before, during, and after completing the item?

4. Reward yourself after the completion of each Big Task with a break, such as checking social media or getting a snack.

5. Catch yourself getting distracted. Notice when you begin to stray from your desired feeling. If you get irritated or stressed, move on to a different task. Better yet, take a movement break.

Case Study: Claire

Let's look at a case study on shifting from fixing a problem to accepting the situation and seeing what new possibilities arise.

Twelve years ago, Claire gained 50 pounds after having her first child and never lost the baby weight. She has tried various cleanses, diets, and nutrition plans that resulted in temporary weight loss. Inevitably, the stress of life crept back in and she returned to the cycle of binge eating and bashing herself for regaining weight.

Anyone else familiar with the yo-yo dieting?

Food is not the problem. Claire's issue may be a feeling of inadequacy. Until she can feel whole, healthy, and complete in herself, she will continue to reach for food or wine or whatever she likes to get the short hit of dopamine.

Hugs, massages, baths, meditation, and listening to music are all activities that boost feel-good chemicals in the body in a more sustainable way. But who has time for all that, right? Claire wakes up and immediately starts thinking of all the things she has to do: make breakfast, get the kids to school, run to the store to get snacks for the soccer team, go to work, and so on.

1. She pauses and remembers gratitude. Placing her hands over her heart, she says, *I am grateful for . . .*

   My healthy body

   My partner who loves and supports me

   The cute smile on my son's face while he sleeps

   The smell of fresh coffee

   The sunlight on the windowsill

   The running water in the bathroom

   The teachers who give so much to my kids

   Our dog who is always happy

   A full pantry to feed the family

   A warm bed to sleep in

2. Then she asks herself, *How shall I be of greatest service today? What would serve the highest good of all?* First, she makes a list of 3 Big Tasks:

   Big Task #1. Call three clients and thank them for their business

   Big Task #2. Log all the purchases from last month in my accounting software program

   Big Task #3: Write a new blog post

3. Then, for each Big Task, she assigns a desired feeling or outcome:
    a. Gratitude for referrals or feedback
    b. Focused and calm to get organized and clear
    c. Creative and exuberant to write a captivating blog

4. After completing Big Task #1, calling three clients, Claire takes a break to check text messages and social media.

5. Then she starts posting on social media. An hour is gone, and she starts to feel anxious because she feels like she isn't progressing like her friends on social media.

6. It's time to reboot and take a walk, meditate, or eat a healthy meal.

7. Claire moves on to Big Task #2, logging all her purchases into her accounting software program. *Aaack! I don't like accounting,* she thinks. Then Claire catches herself and flips her thinking around to: *I am so happy and grateful that I have enough income to make these purchases for my business.* She sets a timer for 30 minutes and completes this task in that time frame.

8. When Big Task #2 is complete, she has a dance party to get juiced up and ready to write that blog post.

9. She sets the timer again, this time for 60 minutes to write the blog. She is amazed at how efficiently she gets things done in the time she's allowed herself. And Claire knows that if she doesn't get the tasks done, it is okay.

Multitasking is a fallacy. Stop trying to do everything all at once. Instead, slow down, take a breath, and express gratitude. Break down your tasks, give yourself time and space to complete each one, reward yourself when you complete a task, and know that it is okay when you do not finish a particular task within your goal time.

It is so easy to slip back into multi-tasking. I revert back to it frequently but with practice you will become clearer, more focused. Your body and your mind will operate more efficiently when you slow down.

Stop Hating on Yourself

You are a being of Divine perfection. Your body is a temple that carries your soul through this lifetime. I beg you, Mom, to begin treating yourself like the goddess that you are.

Stop saying, *I hate my* _____. (Fill in the blank with ass, thighs, eyebrows, toenails, etc.)

What do you love about yourself? Make as long a list as you can.

For example, *I love my eyes. I love the way my eyes glimmer when I am smiling wholeheartedly.*

What if you spent all day being in your body with wonder, awe, and amazement instead of loathing, fear, and shame?

If you ever doubt the beauty of your feminine form, look through the annals of art history. What we would label fat or chubby today was revered in the 1600s as voluptuous and beautiful. The standards for your beauty don't have to be dictated by a magazine. Start claiming yourself as the radiant goddess that you are. (If goddess isn't your kind of word, fill in the blank with whatever you feel is most empowering -- badass, woman, flower, etc.)

If you are wound up and doing something all the time, how are you going to be still and receive anything that is new, bright, and beyond your wildest dreams?

When I first separated from my former spouse and for about three years after, my life was in upheaval. My children adapted more quickly than I did as they moved back and forth, from one house to another, each with its different values, standards, and daily routines.

My son explained to me today how he prepares himself for going to his dad's house. He said he likes to start getting his bag packed a couple of days ahead of time so he feels prepared and less stressed when it's time to switch homes. He is 10 and is learning self-regulation.

I am still learning how to self-regulate amid the whirlwind of activities:

> carting kids to therapy appointments,
>
> fielding yet another call from school about my son skipping class,
>
> attending the court's intervention and restorative justice programs for my son,
>
> running a household,
>
> marketing and promoting my business,
>
> following up with customers,
>
> closing sales,
>
> coaching calls and networking groups, and
>
> going to school meetings and doctor appointments.

I always find time for myself.

My kids have been learning all along the way. Truthfully, their transformation from chaos to harmony happened as I began to do less.

It goes back to that old saying I mentioned earlier, *If Mama ain't happy, no one is.*

Hey, Moms:

You are responsible for your own happiness. No one else can make you happy. You cannot blame anyone else for your unhappiness, either.

Really, Gina? Are you saying I have to own my shit?

Yes, you need to acknowledge your weaknesses. And then love those parts of yourself just like you would love your wailing infant.

You may want to avoid facing your inadequacies by covering them or hiding from the truth. You may want to put bandages over them and continue with the frantic pace of life -- because that's more productive, right? But just like a baby with a pacifier, eventually, the deeper needs take over, and the baby is wailing again because she is hungry or has a dirty diaper.

Meanwhile, owning your shit does not mean you take the awareness of yourself and use it as ammunition to beat yourself up or give yourself a hard time.

Your so-called flaws are here to teach you, but you must slow down and become receptive. First, notice yourself, and then love yourself exactly where you are.

Although self-love practices take time to integrate into your day, the obligations that strip you of your desired feelings begin to fall away as you take time to love yourself even more.

Wouldn't it be nice if you could go to the convenience store to pick up a self-love kit? But there are no quick fixes. It takes a willingness to slow down and just be.

Being busy all the time is a recipe for a myriad of stress-related illnesses, such as heart attacks, cancer, and autoimmune disorders. Living a healthy, fulfilled life is far more important than staying busy and occupying yourself with activities that disrupt your inner balance.

It takes time to love yourself. The first hurdle is to stop letting time manage you.

What we call obstacles are really how the world and our entire experience teach us where we're stuck.

~ *Pema Chodron*[1]

Time to Love Yourself

Which to you sounds more relaxing? Sitting on a runway with airplanes taking off every 30 seconds and jet fuel fumes in your nose, or sitting in your bathtub with warm water, Epsom salts, and soft music? I would guess most of you chose the latter.

Isn't living in chaos more like scenario one? Why would we ever voluntarily choose chaos when peace and presence are always available to us?

Must the monetary rewards of hard work always overshadow the deep soul gifts of living from the heart?

How can you serve the world from your heart when you are constantly in motion, never allowing yourself to be replenished and refueled?

Being a receiver is different from being a mooch or sitting on your laurels waiting for something to happen. The difference is that when your actions come from a heart-centered, soulful place, you have more power and impact in the world. You no longer need to run at breakneck speed on the treadmill of life because you will be propelling the journey instead of pacing with the conveyor belt beneath you. Being intentional is your first step towards being in control of your life. Exercise, for example, doesn't happen unless you resolve to do it. That email or text can wait. Show up and stick to what motivates and inspires YOU first!

You may be thinking that I have lost touch with what it's like to be a mother of infants and toddlers. There is simply no time for me, moms of young ones might say. Sure, my kids' ages are all in double digits now. But as I reflect on those younger, chaotic years, I wish I had understood what I am now presenting in this book.

If I had spent half as much time grounding myself and taking care of myself as I did reading parenting books and feeling like I was doing the wrong thing because my kids didn't respond to the methods outlined in those books, my life would have been so much easier.

In 2016, I discovered Dr. Shefali Tsabary's book, *The Awakened Family: A Revolution in Parenting*. This book forever changed the way I would parent.

> *We cannot control our children. We can only create the conditions for them to rise. What this means is that we need to stop expending our energy on trying to control who they are and how they turn out in the future. The real challenge is to keep our eyes on the parameters that are truly under our control -- ourselves, and the way the home functions.*
>
> *~ Dr. Shefali Tsabary[2]*

For any parent attached to the authoritarian model of parenting, i.e., my way or the highway, Tsabary's book is blasphemy. I mean, how can we possibly control our kids if we aren't focusing on setting boundaries and limits and holding them to those standards with a system of rewards and punishments?

All I can tell you is that as I let go of the need to monitor and control my kids' phone usage and screen time and as I stop punishing or taking things away in response to undesirable behavior, my children have begun to respect me more.

By demonstrating better self-control, asking more questions, and becoming more engaged in their world instead of trying to guide them into the direction that society says they should go, I have begun to cultivate a home that encourages sovereign, joyful, independent beings.

I still lose my temper, but I catch myself quicker now because nothing is worth losing my peace of mind. For example, the other day, the boys were kicking the soccer ball in the basement. I am getting ready to sell my home, so I am hypervigilant about keeping the house in order. I heard a loud crash, and the walls shook.

I yelled from upstairs, "What in the hell is going on down there?!!"

And then I took a deep breath, went downstairs, and inquired calmly, "What just happened? I heard a loud sound."

"It's okay, Mom," my youngest reassured me. "I bumped into the wall, but everything is okay."

"Please be mindful of where you kick the ball," I replied and resumed cooking.

I trust that my kids know my standards and values now that they are beyond 10 years old. And when they fall short, I know it is not my fault. They get to take responsibility for their actions.

During the pandemic's remote-learning times, I received daily calls from the attendance line at my son's high school. He logged in when he was ready to start his day, and he got his stuff done. And when he didn't, that was on him, NOT me.

It has been difficult raising a child who sees school as a waste of time. Now he is getting ready to take his GED test after passing all the pre-tests. Credit-wise, he is a sophomore, yet his test scores reflect that he can now test out of community college courses.

Taking the GED is not the path I would have liked for him to go down, but now that I am accepting it, there is less conflict between us.

Take Responsibility for Your Life

When you are living a chaotic life, you may hear yourself say things like:

I am so overwhelmed.

There isn't enough time in the day.

If only I had more time (or another set of arms, etc.).

You have more control when you are calm and centered. From a place of peace, you can make wiser choices, pivot more easily, and recover more quickly from setbacks. Sure, it's easier to blame your crazed life on your schedule, the dog, the house, or your spouse. Taking responsibility for your life requires stepping off the treadmill of life and deciding how and when you will take action to maintain or reclaim your desired feelings.

Now, how the heck do you even know what your desired feelings are when chaos and calamity is all you know?

Let Desire Lead the Way

When I work with my personal training clients, I have found that using a goal-setting approach is ineffective in the long term and produces only temporary results. People become too focused on an external result and often become disappointed when they do not meet the goal. Instead, I ask them, *What do you desire? If you could wave a magic wand and create your ideal life, what would it look like for you six months from now?*

I find that many moms have lost touch with what they desire. It is almost like the aspiration to be a good mom and fulfill their children's dreams has overshadowed their own.

Let's go through the process I use to help you find your desired feeling state.

1. Journal. Set a timer for five minutes, start writing with the prompt, *I desire ...* and let your pen run wild.

2. Observe yourself as you write. Are you resistant? Do you feel confused? Are you having fun with it? Are you drawing a blank? If you cannot get past it, come back to writing later. Take a walk. Do something you enjoy. You will be tempted to avoid this writing prompt claiming, *I don't know what I want!* You might hear a voice. *It doesn't matter what I desire. I am too busy to take time for myself.* If all your obligations were lifted, what is the life you would desire?

   Another option is to keep writing without screening your words. Just let the pen flow. You know in your heart of hearts what you want. Maybe 5 minutes is too short. Write for 10 minutes if you still don't harvest the gold.

3. Do you yearn for a deeper sense of You? Reread your writing and highlight the words that light you up. Make a list of those words. Feel each word in your body and place a star next to your top three.

4. Now write each of the three words on separate cards or sticky notes. Post them in a variety of locations you will easily see... a bathroom mirror, over the kitchen sink, and on your car dashboard.

5. Write a statement. I claim _____, _____, and _____ for my life from now on. Speak, "I claim

health, happiness and harmony for my life from now on!" out loud. Words have vibration and when you speak you activate that positive potential into reality.

6. When you find yourself steering away from the feelings of those words, notice that you feel off the wagon, so to speak. Then say to yourself, "I reclaim health for my life right now!"

7. Look for evidence of your words showing up in your life and write them down daily in a gratitude journal.

Notice the words *frenzied, chaotic,* and *stressed* are not on the list. Do you often find yourself telling people you are overwhelmed, busy or stressed? This does not have to be your natural way of being a mom. Change your core belief or perception of yourself from stressed to stable or from overwhelmed to in harmony and you will begin to tune into and attract more flow and ease into your life, naturally.

I know it seems tantalizing and attractive to brag about the endless list of activities that you do, but the last time I checked, there is no award for being the busiest mom on the block.

When you understand your desired feelings and start leading with the longing to be that kind of woman in the world, you will begin to attract opportunities where you can be in your essence. That is a beautiful, inspired way to live.

It is natural to have doubts about letting go of structure and routine as your guiding parameters. If your current routine and way of doing things spark your desired feelings, then keep at it. I have found that most people walk mindlessly through their days when locked into uninspiring, rote routines.

Routine is the mother of monotony, and monotony can lead to chaotic living because you are reacting rather than responding to life.

Routine vs. Ritual

Rituals add a quality of the sacred to your day. Every moment is a gift to behold. When I fall into routines or ruts, I feel mindless, and my actions lack inspiration.

Let's go back to the question, *How do I want to feel?*

While I may be trying to get into the routine of writing 2,000 words per day, I will not force it if the inspiration is not there. When I fall into a rut, I pause and ask myself, *How do I want to feel right now?*

I assure you the answer is never, *Angry, frustrated, fearful, and deluded.* And yet that is how I felt prior to opening my laptop this morning.

I could have said to myself like a relentless coach of an Olympian, *No excuses. Sit your ass down and start writing. The day is wasting.*

Instead, I set a parameter around the reboot time: *I will give myself until 10 a.m. to get my head on straight. In the meantime, I am going to rage and feel the frustration and know that the fear I feel could also be perceived as excitement. I am scared as hell as I write this book, knowing from my deepest core being that these words must be written, and I must share my story for so many moms who are struggling right now in these times of pandemonium.*

And so here we are all strung out with the trauma of being isolated trying to operate and function at the same speed, attending meetings, going to fundraisers, helping kids with homework, working or running a business, managing a household, refereeing a number of daily arguments.... Oh, and did somebody say something about self-care?

Time for Self Care

Who has TIME for self-care? I'll take a bubble bath. There, I did my self-care. Now I'll post it on Facebook with bubbles sparkling and a glass of wine waiting on the bathtub rim.

Ahhh...this is the life, you might write in your post.

Then, you enter the bathtub, and your mind-switch flips on and you worry about all the things you didn't do to make time for this bath you're running.

And then there is the sound of children bickering down below.

You say to yourself, *Ignore it! I told them to only bother me if there was blood or injury involved.*

Does it make me a bad mom for making my health and well-being a priority while my kids are duking it out?

Obviously, if your kids are younger, use nap time or after bedtime for YOU time instead of seeing how much you can get done during those opportune times.

I can hear my mother, Sharon, saying to me, "When the baby naps, you lie down and rest, too."

I would roll my eyes and say, "Yes, mom. I get it." And in the back of my mind I thought, *Moms today are so much tougher. We don't need nap time.*

I was one of those moms who viewed nap time as a time to see how much I could get done. Ready. Set. Go. I am sure I ran myself into adrenal fatigue, a lay term for a disease state that results from chronic stress. The adrenal glands release hormones when we are exposed to stress, and when this pressure is chronic, the adrenal function diminishes. This can result in insomnia, rage, loss of appetite and depression. To this day, I continue to recover from the massive nervous system damage I incurred.

Before I discovered the power of ritual, I would push through everything in the name of keeping up with the routine. In those days, I would spout off at every spilled cup of milk and broken glass. And then every little thing for the rest of my day would create a huge uproar.

The Effects of Stress

When the brain senses a threat albeit real (a car cuts you off in traffic) or perceived (you can't find your keys and you are late for work), a flood of hormones is released into the bloodstream within 10 seconds of the triggering event. In those 10 seconds, we can stave off the stress by taking a deep belly breath or by asking a powerful question, such as, *How can I stay calm in this moment?* Why is it so important to prevent the release of the stress hormones cortisol and adrenaline? Once the cortisol enters the bloodstream, it takes nine hours for men and a whopping 24 hours for women to process the cortisol out of the body.

I never knew this fact until I began working with Elle Ingalls, the founder of the Pressure-Free Method and author of the book, *Pressure-Free Parenting: The Ten Second Solution to Less Stress and Anxiety for High-Achieving Families*, I hired Elle for her Jump Start program during the stressful summer of 2019 when my oldest son would regularly run away for days at a time and go on drug binges.

Ingalls spent an entire 90-minute session teaching me about the physiology of stress. I learned that adrenaline and cortisol, when left unchecked, can cause the following disruptions in the body's function[3]:

- Weakened immune function
- Slowed digestion

- Insomnia
- Achy joints/inflammation
- Slower metabolism
- Blood sugar imbalance
- Increased blood pressure
- Brain and neuron damage
- Increased abdominal fat
- Slower Healing
- Muscle and bone loss

And the list goes on.

The stress response is designed to protect us when we are in the face of a real threat to our survival, but, unfortunately, the brain cannot distinguish between an unpleasant memory and being held at gunpoint.

I would speculate that most moms are under constant attack by the stress hormones in the body. We can literally never catch a breath. Weight gain, chronic illness, fatigue, coffee addiction, joint pain, and compromised immune function are just a few symptoms of the body's breakdown under chronic stress.

The insidious nature of the stress response is that over time, an individual may lose her ability to manage the response effectively, and she becomes a rage machine day after day and eventually, every cell in the body deteriorates and loses optimal function.

In the beginning, when I started to use Elle's *9 Tools to Stop Stress*, I had a difficult time catching the stress in time but I became mindful of what precipitated the stress. At first, I would celebrate when I could make it half a day without raging and these days I can go days and weeks at a time without instigating a stress response.

And to think that every single day, most moms experience unprecedented levels of stress. It's no wonder why moms in their 30s are already showing early signs of chronic illness and aging, such as diabetes, autoimmune disorder, and inflammation gone wild. The stress hormones are literally weakening the body and making it more susceptible to disease.

It breaks my heart to see young mothers in and out of clinics receiving testing, then getting treatments that never seem to cure the cause. What if the cure was slowing down and taking on less responsibility?

Remember, 90% of illness has its roots in stress.

So the question is, *Can you afford NOT to slow down?*

Can you afford to keep going at warp speed as hospital bills and prescription-drug expenses begin to accrue?

Could it be that doing less is MORE?

Healthy Living is Easy

I use a valuable medical device that increases blood circulation by 30%. I lie on the mat for eight minutes twice daily, and voila, I achieve blood flow comparable to taking two 30-minute jogs each day. The signal is delivered via an electromagnetic field. I rarely feel anything at all when I am using it, but the signal stimulates the release of nitric oxide, which in turn greatly increases the delivery of nutrients and oxygen to the cells and enhances waste removal, too.

It has been my easy go-to for most of my health challenges over the last 5 years.

Even though my body has resolved all its aches and physical limitations since I began using it four years ago.

Even though I have navigated the last four tumultuous years of upheaval with relative ease and grace, logging zero sick days in the process.

Even though I have been able to maintain calm amidst most parents' worst nightmares.

People still can't believe that lying on a mat twice daily could make such an impact on one's health and well-being. Most of them are overlooking the value of fully nourished cells free from excess waste. Some people may feel calmer the first time using the device while for others, they may have to use it for several months before realizing the benefits. Scientific studies show that the increase in circulation is immediate and lasts up to15 hours.

There is no other modality on the market today that can log this level of sustained blood flow.

It was a substantial investment. When I look at the way I have been able to thrive through this extremely stressful time in my life and also the business opportunity it provided me to earn extra money as a sales distributor for the company, I know I made an important investment that will continue to deliver great health benefits for many years to come.

The truth is, the most impactful work the body does is in the recovery phase. For example, you might read a book or learn a new skill. If you never slept, the brain would never be able to process the new information. Have you ever tried to take a test after pulling an all nighter? You probably struggled to come up with the answers. Similarly, when the body is fatigued, you are more susceptible to injury and illness.

We live in a culture that is stepping out of the no-pain-no-gain mentality and into a less mechanical flow state. Interest in yoga and meditation is on the rise. Recovery modalities like hyperbaric chambers and pulsing massage guns are becoming more commonplace. Facilities that offer oxygen bars and IV infusions and salt caves are trending. People know they have to corral their stress.

So, I ask, would you rather use something like the electromagnetic device and lie still twice daily for eight minutes or cram pills, coffee, and wine down your mouth and hope for something better that never seems to come?

Don't get me wrong. Even if you lie on this device, you still have to maintain a relatively healthy diet, drink good-quality water, and move your body.

My point is, living healthy can be easy. Modern biotechnology is making it easier than ever to maintain homeostasis even while environmental toxins and fast paced lifestyles present a challenge to living a healthy life.

You cannot thrive on chaos unless you have a resilient, well-trained nervous system like an ER doctor. After an animal has fled a predator, you often will observe it shaking it off and moving on. What if you, too, could shake off stress within a 10-second window?

Remember, you have a 10-second time frame to avoid the hormone-induced stress response. So, instead of losing your peace when agitated, do this instead, PLEASE.

Take a deep breath

soften your abs and

ask...how can I communicate better with my son?

Even though I teach and practice yoga and meditation, I still struggle with slowing down. I get caught up in the task lists and the pandemonium, too.

I am quick to recognize it, and I am getting better and better at staying out of the dark pit of my mind.

A little hack never hurts anyone, especially in these times when we are being bludgeoned with wifi signals, toxic chemicals, and extreme information overload. We cannot escape these things but we can use tools like meditation, music, eating healthy, and staying active to counter these negative effects.

I call my magic machine a bio-hack, because it does in eight minutes what sometimes requires much longer for me to feel in 30 minutes of meditation.

What if you could do more with less?

What if you could make a bigger impact without adding more to your already full plate?

What if the chaos were a swirl around you and you only stepped into it voluntarily with your wits about you?

But how can you keep your wits about you when there is so much uncertainty and so much concern for health and safety these days?

At the time of this writing, grocery shopping is a carefully planned and plotted activity.

You grab the mask and maybe the gloves and then disinfect everything upon entering and leaving the building.

Spray and sanitize all the bags.

Then wash your hands and everyone else's the minute you enter the door.

And when you add the screaming, pent-up child to the cart, you have the recipe for a perfect meltdown for both mom and child.

I get it, Mom! Life can be stressful. That is why you MUST, MUST, MUST put your health at the forefront of your priorities.

Start each day from a place of inspiration rather than obligation and watch how life begins to flow.

Lest I digress, let's return to ritual as the foundation for living your inspired life.

Living an Inspired Life

I created a program called *21 Practices to Inspire Your Life*. Each day over the course of 21 days, I send out short daily practices to participants to inspire deeper, heart-centered daily living. On one day, I may ask members to do something that scares them and then ask how doing that affected them. On another day, I invite the community to spend the day making themselves right about everything. And on yet another day, we each take a slow walk in nature. We join together in community to cultivate love, harmony, and connection. And that, in itself, is inspiring.

Our external circumstances may not change, but we can still choose to live inspired lives rather than lives based on lack and fear. And we, in turn, model for our children a healthier way of living that expands us rather than shuts us down.

In my first run of the program, I watched how each one of the moms responded in her own way. A couple of moms were right there, responding to daily posts and practicing daily. From others, I heard nothing. And there were those who took what they could use and left the rest behind.

Overall, I love that the 21 Practices evoked insights from the moms. Here are just two examples of what they told me:

> "I discovered there is no badge of honor for being busy. Being busy is a mark of success in our culture, and I am stepping away from that to find more meaning in my life." ~ Veronica S.

"I find that just by taking five minutes a day for me, I can build my day on a more solid, sustainable foundation and be an even better mom to my daughters."
~ Meg S.

You see, when the alarm says go and we hit the ground running, we are always catching up with the day. But the days begin to flow when you decide to begin the day consciously, rather than scrolling the morning social media feed right away. Instead ask for guidance from a place of heartfelt gratitude and watch what happens.

I am living proof. I had to harmonize my own inner life and step out of the chaos that accompanied my broken marriage.

Creating peace and harmony at home began when I chose to take a bath at 2 p.m. instead of making more phone calls. Building family bonds happened when I stopped listening to webinars through dinnertime. When I began to accept that my oldest son was on his own path and there was little I could do or say to sway him, I began to envision his success instead of lamenting his failures. That practice of acceptance dampened the feelings of shame that I had felt about his situation and paved the way for love to lead the way.

Cultivating love at home began when I stopped taking on more than I could handle. (That is still a work in progress.)

Being (as one client described me) the "greeter goddess to the mama tribe and queen of finding joy in movement," I pride myself in finding the way out of chaos into my highest and best self. I want that for you, too, Mom. You are a regal goddess of infinite love. Treat yourself as the magnificent queen that you are. Sit on your throne and adore your life. Create the new story that you are masterfully mindful rather than a master multitasker. You will be amazed by how simple your life becomes.

Chapter Three

Myth #3: Being a Mom Is Tough

Myth-buster: When you say to yourself, being a mom is tough, you will find all kinds of evidence to support that truth.

Reality: Being a mom can be enlightening when you view challenges as learning opportunities.

It's true that there is a lot to juggle as a mom. I used to fully embrace the *I thrive on chaos* and *I love to stay busy* mindsets.

As I explained in Myth #2, when we are stressed, we experience the following:

Impaired judgment

Memory lapses

Negative thoughts

Insomnia

Doesn't it stand to reason that in our impaired, stressed-out state of brain fog, our ability to accomplish tasks efficiently is diminished?

I know I made countless foolish decisions in my state of anxiety-induced brain stupor. For example, there was the debt elimination company that contacted me shortly after my divorce was finalized.

Strapped with debt and in a newly financed mortgage, I had no idea how I would make the monthly payments on the four credit cards. I prayed about it and waited for the answers to come. So when the debt relief company called me and offered a way out, I naively interpreted that as Divine intervention.

Without going into detail about a story that I am ashamed to recount, suffice it to say that the company was a scam. My credit was in shambles for years to come.

Had I felt safe and secure in the world and, as a result, had a calm and regulated nervous system, I might have taken time to research the legitimacy of the company. Because the reaction to stress impairs judgment, I can likely attribute more unfortunate decisions to the state of calamity in my life.

Calling the Cops

My son was pounding on my locked bathroom door, demanding, "Give me my phone back!"

I was on the phone with my good friend. Sensing my panic, she called a crisis hotline to assist me.

On the phone, the counselor asked me, "Is that your son yelling at you?"

"Yes!" I cried nervously.

To a teenage boy who had been a victim of abuse, bullying and force were what he knew.

My son continued to threaten to break down the door even when I placed the crisis counselor on speakerphone to talk with him.

The counselor, hearing his persistent threats, advised me to call the cops for a safety check. I resisted. "No! We are not involving the cops."

She called them anyway, and that first visit from the police became the first of dozens of peacekeeping calls to the local sheriff's office I would initiate in my moments of panic and duress over the next three years.

As a single mom, I was trying, unsuccessfully, to be both Mom and Dad. My kids were used to the "wait till your Dad gets home" style of discipline. With Dad out of the picture, I had no idea how to peacefully resolve these conflicts with my son.

I stayed in a constant state of panic and fear, and our relationship deteriorated.

The harder I forced, the further away I pushed my son.

He needed compassion and grace and help to figure out how to regulate his own anxiety. I was no help at all because I was in a constant state of fight or flight.

If I had had better control of myself, would I have repeatedly called the cops to come to my home to get control of my angry and dysregulated teenage son? Would my son have perceived his mother as unable to handle the stress life was throwing her way?

When the fighting began, it would quickly escalate. My son would punch a hole in the wall or grapple me into a headlock. I would call the cops and sometimes file a report. My son's trust in me dwindled with each incident. Eventually, we were caught in a perpetual cycle of lack of trust, expecting the worst from each other.

After more than a dozen calls, I finally asked the cops to take my son to the juvenile assessment center (JAC) for a six-hour hold. What parent ever wants to see her son hauled off in handcuffs? I had no other outlet for relief so the JAC became my safety holding cell on three separate occasions. But the situation did not change, and the relationship between my son and me continued to deteriorate. He lost faith in me because, as he would share with me when he was older, "Instead of connecting with me, you just called the cops to take me away."

The fact is, I didn't feel safe around my son. He made my life a living hell with his persistent lack of respect for my boundaries and house rules.

Truth be told, *I* made my life hell. I chose resistance, tension, and difficulty. That is what chronic stress does to you. You begin to see life through a very narrow lens and always expect the worst.

Until, one day, I had a revelation. Life can be easy, and I could choose ease, comfort, and fun instead of hard work and suffering.

Epiphany on the Stairs

Now that I am consciously choosing pleasure over pain and peace instead of chaos, my life is becoming so much easier. Before I was introduced to the Pressure-Free method of staving off stress, I was anxious most of the time. I was bouncing from one shiny object to the next with no clarity or focus. It felt like the executive function of my brain had completely shut down.

NO WONDER LIFE WAS SO HARD!

One morning, as I prepared to run up the 200 stairs at Red Rocks Amphitheater (which always kicks my ass), I looked up and said to myself, *Today, running the stairs will be easy.*

I took a deep breath and softened my abs. (Did you know that when the abs are tight, it sends a *you are not safe* signal to the brain? By letting the belly feel like a bowl full of jello, we can actually move more efficiently.)

During my ascent, each time I felt my body tense up, I proclaimed, *This is easy!* And my body would relax. At the top, when I tapped *stop* on my timer, I rejoiced that I had cut three seconds off my previous best time, a significant improvement.

Thinking it a fluke, I repeated the ascent three more times. As expected, each run took a little longer. But the fact that I kept the overall increase to under 10 seconds is remarkable.

I began to reflect on how I could apply this method to other aspects of my life. I mean, what if being a mom could be easy? I would listen to my body and rest when it feels tense. Instead of scolding my children for bad behavior, I would ask questions to seek out reasons for their actions. Before I could shift into ease, I had to notice my current way of being.

Increasingly, I began to notice my bullish (I am a Taurus) tendency to push through everything. I found myself often depleted and overwhelmed from constantly forcing myself.

You never have to force what is truly meant to be.

~ Cynthia Gardner O'Neill

From Anxiety to Tranquility

Have you ever forced yourself to get your taxes done before the deadline? Or do you consistently push yourself to exercise? In both cases, not fun, right?

When we are constantly forcing, chasing, and pursuing, the body cannot rest.

Have you ever noticed that your actions are less productive when you force things? When I was the Wellness Program Administrator for a city recreation department, I prepared dozens of pages of budget spreadsheets. I had a deadline and, of course, I put the project off until the last minute. It would come as no surprise when my boss found several big errors that messed up the other projections I had made.

In fact, most aspects of my responsible management job left me feeling depleted mentally and emotionally. Why? I hated doing desk work and administration, yet as an administrator, that was a large aspect of my work.

After years of working on my feet as a trainer and group fitness instructor in a gym, the constant sitting and left-brain activity of this new role presented a predicament. How could I utilize my creative right brain in a position where following steps, safety codes, and protocols was the highest priority?

Within one month of taking on this new job, I gained 10 pounds; within three months, I was taking antidepressants. According to societal norms, I had finally made it! Never before as a personal trainer had I been offered a benefits package with health insurance, vision, and dental coverage. Retirement savings. Vacation time. Sick days. Steady income. My family celebrated that I had finally made it to the management level, but my body was clearly communicating dissatisfaction.

Had I sold my soul for stability?

My parents visited about a year into my tenure at this job. My dad sat across from me and said, "Gina, you are not happy." I agreed with him. How could I feel so unhappy with such a responsible, steady job?

Within a month after the conversation with my father, I quit my job. That was in 2014, and ever since then, I have been pursuing my dream of running my own business.

And that has been a journey of ups, downs, twists, and turns. Being a business owner is tough. What if running a successful business merely required being myself so fully and completely that my authenticity became the factor that attracted people easily into my sphere? I have worked with a half dozen business coaches and I have diligently attended as many sales seminars as I could muster. It wasn't until recently when I learned to relax and allow others to have their own experience and stop pushing my agenda onto others that clients began to ask me for my services. By showing up as myself, the good, the bad, and the ugly, I have shown others by example that it is possible to thrive through difficult times. In fact, thriving only happens when there is something tough to overcome. I have demonstrated that challenges strengthen us when we lead with love instead of needing to fix ourselves.

Starting a business requires wearing many hats. I have learned about marketing, sales, social media, client retention, management, and writing good copy. And I have been raising a family, getting divorced, and putting myself back together all at the same time.

It has become increasingly clear to me that I cannot be a mom, website designer, bookkeeper, marketing expert, domestic engineer, partner, and friend. No way! In my push to pursue and do things that are not my expertise, I have built three different websites to no avail. I have been on a quest to find my ideal client. I have spent tens of thousands of dollars on coaches and websites only to build and rebuild my offerings over and over again.

After many mishaps like this, I decided I had to change my stubborn ways. Perhaps things like budgets and marketing reports would have taken less time had I approached them with peace and joy in my heart instead of dread and disgust.

Ask for Help

Doing it all implies that no one can do it better or that everything will fall apart if you aren't participating in a task. It is actually a very self-centered way of living, and it is tough, too.

I have observed that most people love to be of service. When you receive the gift of service, you are actually giving the receiver the gift of feeling useful.

Your helpers may not always do things exactly to your standards, though. There are dozens of ways to do the dishes, for instance. If you insist that it must be done your way, then you might as well do it yourself and alleviate the drain of frustration.

As a single mom entrepreneur playing many roles, I had to quickly delegate tasks to more effectively offer my services to the world. When I ask the kids to clean the bathroom, I have to expect that there will be a few hairs left in the sink. When they fold the clothes, the fold lines may not be clean and crisp. And so it is.

Good Enough

My mom subscribes to Good Housekeeping magazine. I remember a column where they would feature a cleaning task, then show the *Good Enough*, *Good*, and *Deep Clean* versions of the chore.

I find myself opting more and more for the *good enough* version of each task, where I might, for example, sweep the kitchen floor without moving all the chairs out of the way.

On another day, I will be jamming to Prince in my kitchen and get a burst of energy that drives me to move all the items off the floor and do a deep clean with a broom and mop.

It feels so much better to approach a task when you want to do it. If you don't want to and you have to, then by all means find a way to make it fun. What gets your juices flowing? Music, artwork, and the promise of a reward are all ways to create ease and flow in the completion of your tasks.

Anchoring the Light

> *If you are anchoring the Light from your soul, it doesn't exhaust you.*
>
> ~ Matt Kahn

You might be familiar with the term, anchoring the light. But what exactly does this mean? When we approach life with heartfelt intentionality instead of logical rationality, we tend to make choices that naturally align with us energetically. Leading with the question, *How do I want to feel?* helps us feel lit up and fulfilled. In contrast, when I ask the question, *What should I do?* I feel obligated and that is draining.

What do you currently do that exhausts you? Does thinking about it zap your energy? Ask yourself: Is it something you can delegate? Is it essential? If it is your responsibility and it has to be done, let's turn it into a sacred ritual.

For instance, why not light some incense in the bathroom before you clean the toilet and tub? Say a prayer and ask the bathroom angels to bless this space and make it a temple of peace. I know many parents of toddlers use the commode as the only place for solitude sometimes. Might as well make it sacred space, right?

When cooking dinner, what if you blessed yourself and the food you are about to prepare. You might say something like this: *Thank you for this food. Bring calm into my heart so that I may prepare this meal with love and cultivate harmony in my home with the presentation of this meal.*

Have yard work to do? Have you ever expressed gratitude for the grass that has grown so long it must be cut? What if pulling weeds could become a meditation on the things in your own life that would be better to extract so you can enhance your growth potential?

Anchoring the light in simple daily tasks or chores brings meaning and reverence to what could otherwise be rote duty

Being the Light

When I was an exhausted mom, every day I would tell myself, *I am not going to yell at the kids today.* One day, my son and I were baking cookies. He knocked over my cup of chai on the kitchen counter where I had precariously perched it on the four inches of counter space around the sink. I screamed when the spicy dairy drink fell to the ground. It was completely not my son's fault, and yet I made a big deal about how I was taking time from my workday, and now we had to clean it all up.

In a calmer, more clear-headed state, maybe I would have laughed at myself for being so foolish to leave my cup where I did. Maybe I would have recognized that in my agitated state, I didn't need the caffeine anyway.

I used to pride myself on my ability to push through my days with less than three hours of sleep. I was a walking time bomb, yelling and screaming over spilled chai. Now, I take a midafternoon rest. I allow myself to miss deadlines in favor of keeping my sanity. And the whole household is happier as a result. I can regulate my reactions and respond instead.

Creating time and space for a morning ritual is a key element. It varies from day to day but I always make time to ask Spirit for guidance. One day, I might do yoga and meditation. Another day, I may put on music and dance and then journal. There is always a way to wake up and celebrate that my body is healthy, whole, and complete.

I can now recognize when worry grips me. Instead of fretting, I ask a powerful question, such as, *What can I do instead of worry about money?* Or, *How can I be of service to my family, my community, and to the world at large?*

When I am tied up in knots and running in circles, there is no way to see the bigger picture.

One Easter, my youngest son cut his finger. Blood was spurting everywhere. While I was bracing myself and breathing deeply as I prepared to look at the cut, my oldest was already helping clean the wound, while saying to me, "Mom, I got this. Calm down."

Worry is so difficult to avoid when parenting. There are so many things to be concerned about. Will my kids encounter a child predator? Will they get onto incriminating websites or listen to promiscuous music?

And then there are the toddler worries. What if he swallows something, chokes, and dies? What if he lets go of my hand and runs off in the parking lot?

Isn't it true we tend to go to the worst-case scenario?

When my son cut himself, it seemed at the time that he was surely going to have part of his finger amputated. In the end, they glued his cut back together and it healed in a matter of weeks.

The truth is, we make parenting tough because we focus on the tough aspects. What if instead of projecting false conclusions based on worst-case scenario thinking, we approached a problem with anticipation of receiving a brilliant answer? Saying to yourself, I wonder how I will resolve my son's anxiety and fear of meeting new people, will prompt you to seek out help and look for solutions. In contrast, worrying might bring about thoughts like, my son will never amount to anything because he is too shy to talk to anyone. Where have I gone wrong?

Albert Einstein said, "We cannot solve problems with the same thinking that created them."

Asking for assistance from a divine power or from your higher mind, anchored in the light, will yield brilliant solutions.

Parenting teenagers is tough but it is also incredibly enlightening. I learn so much by watching my teens expand their horizons.

I used to cringe at the rap music my oldest son would listen to. The more I protested, the louder he played it. I worried that the profuse profanity and misogynistic messages he heard would damage his psyche and cause him to disrespect women.

One night, I sat down with him and we watched a couple of hours of YouTube videos by his favorite rap artists. Watching with an open mind, I asked him questions. "What do you think of the way they refer to women as 'bitches'?

"Aw. It's just the way they talk, Mom. It don't mean any harm."

"Really," I protested. "As a woman, I don't like being referred to as a bitch or a ho."

After watching one sexist video after another, a song caught my eye: Lil Uzi Vert singing "That's a Rack." The female body, to me, is a work of art. This video accentuates the feminine form with violins, cellos, and other string instruments adorning each woman's body. I could overlook the sexually explicit lyrics because of the artistic arrangement of the video.

That night, I connected with my son and took a trip inside his world. He appreciated that, and he will certainly remember that interaction. I learned from my son to open my mind to rap music. He has a good moral compass, and I can trust him to screen his own music. Stated simply, he realizes that the otherwise offensive aspects of the lyrics are more colloquial and less derogatory.

Now that I have let down the restrictions on his music choices, he freely chooses to create playlists of '40s Big Band music and '90s Alternative. When I released my grip and focused on the light within me, my son was able to explore on his own terms.

My youngest (who is 10 now) is venturing into the world of rap music, and I am taking an interest in what he listens to. Isn't it interesting that he always searches for the "clean" version of the songs? He knows my values (probably from listening to me harp on his older brother for so long), and he makes choices that fit within the framework of those values.

I didn't have to teach him to choose more palatable versions of his music or impose rules and restrictions around what he can and cannot listen to. He makes his choices freely. I take an interest in those choices. Then we have conversations about his choices, and I ask my son questions.

Being a Mom Is Enlightening

My kids are my greatest teachers. When I stepped down from the Mom-knows-best pedestal -- and stopped saying things like, "Because I said so!" -- I began to see my sons and daughter as enlightened teachers.

Each person is sent here for a mission of sorts. It is my job as a mom to ensure the safety of my children and to respect their unique purpose on this planet.

In the authoritarian model of parenting, it's my way or the highway. When we try to raise our kids to fit into our image of an ideal child or fit them into our own box, we will encounter push-back from our kids. When we ask questions about our children's choices, we open the door for learning and discussion.

When we raise our kids with respect, we listen, ask questions, and even celebrate when their choices wander outside our comfort zone. Parenting becomes enlightening.

Going Astray

I answered the phone one summer day, and a detective informed me that my son had posted photos of vodka and weed on Snapchat prior to going to a party. At this same party, a girl accused another boy of raping her.

The illicit evidence my son had posted on social media made him a possible accomplice in the case. I decided to keep an open mind, ask questions, and open a dialog.

I had known that kids are under the mistaken impression that their posts go away quickly on Snapchat. In this case, my son saw no harm in the posts and blamed the girl for being promiscuous after drinking. I explained that he could have been held responsible and charged with a crime. Fortunately for my son, law enforcement officials chose to pursue the accused rapist.

After that incident, I confiscated my son's cell phone. He took off and was gone for days. I had no way of contacting him because he had no cell phone. I called the friends whose numbers I had, but no one had seen him. By this time, he was running with a very different crowd than the polite kids he used to be friends with.

I was in the basement caulking the bathtub when I heard the garage door open. Miles walked in. I hadn't seen him in four days.

"Hey mom," he said as if nothing had happened.

"Where have you been?" I inquired, exasperated.

I didn't know whether I should hug him or shake him.

"Do you know how worried I have been?"

"Chill out, Mom. I'm fine," he calmly explained. "I went downtown on the light rail with Emily. Quit freakin'."

"Who is Emily? And why were you going downtown?"

"She's my girlfriend. Why are you freakin'? We were just mobbin' around. I could have called but I don't have a phone, so it's hard to make a call."

In disbelief, I yelled, "You couldn't use her phone to call me? I have been sick with worry."

I assigned him the task of finishing the caulking for me while I collected myself.

The runaway incidents would continue throughout that difficult summer of 2019. There was the time he jumped off his bed and put me in a headlock when I took his vape pen and threw it in the trash. And the time I found his runaway girlfriend asleep on the mattress in our garage. He fled on foot after both of those episodes.

My heart broke each time, and I know for certain that he slept on park benches during one of his extended outings.

I wanted to give him his phone back and stop this maddening manipulation scheme. I was giving my son a good dose of tough love, dammit!

Eventually, a friend would give him an old phone that he could only use for email. So at least I could send him messages and try to track his whereabouts.

You might be asking, *Gina, why didn't you give him the phone back and require him to use one of those tracking apps?*

I had tried putting time limits on his phone when he was on my plan. His phone would automatically disconnect from wifi after a certain time. As with most tech-savvy teens, he was able to buck that system by using wifi hotspots through my cell phone carrier.

And besides, can you imagine if your parents tracked you as a teenager and knew your every move? I know I would have hated that.

So, I walked the perilous road of not knowing where my son was half the time, but I never relented. As long as he continued to misbehave, I kept his cell phone.

In actuality, this choice became more of a punishment to myself than to him. And he knew that.

My life as a parent during this time was extremely difficult. And I just figured I would have to grin and bear it for the next couple of years until he turned 18.

If I knew then what I know now, I would have asked him more questions before taking the phone away: How can you use your cell phone more responsibly in the future? Can you figure out a way to pay your own phone bill? Let's create a plan to make that happen in 60 days.

Isn't it interesting that the authoritarian method of parenting (punish and take away) backfired and made my life more difficult? All that time, I was trying to hold the higher ground, and he was sneaking around underneath me without a care in the world.

I thought I was a badass for standing my ground, but really, I was being obstinate, and I most definitely wasn't standing in my authentic truth, which is love.

A powerful question we can ask ourselves when our kids defy us is "Would I rather be right in this situation or would I rather have love?"

From Punishment to Learning Opportunities

While driving cross country from Colorado to Indiana, I listened to the Wayne Dyer book, *Inspiration: Your Ultimate Calling*. In it, he suggests that as souls, before our birth, we each choose our parents. I was intrigued.

According to Dyer, we choose our parents based on the soul contract we are here to fulfill. So, for example, one soul may have a contract to learn self-acceptance. He might choose parents who were abusive and angry, so he could learn to love himself even more in this lifetime.

When I began to see my children as teachers, I opened to the possibility of not seeing their behavior as wrong or bad. Do I still struggle with this? Of course. I can now observe my kids' actions with a sense of inquiry. Asking questions first opens the door to communication and then expands the possibilities I can see.

My son vapes and knows that I do not allow it at home. He disagrees with me that it is unhealthy and will hurt him. He says it calms his anxiety. While I enforce the rule at home, he will do as he pleases when he is away from home. I can't control that. Hopefully, some of what I have taught him through this restriction and education will lead him to make healthier choices in the future. If not, that is his choice, and I have no control over his future path.

Let's look at my son's vaping from two different parenting perspectives.

1. *What would Tough Mom do?* She sneaks into her son's room and scours it, looking under the bed and in the closets. She takes any vapes or other illicit items she finds and throws them in the trash. The next day, no surprise; she smells the vaping in her home again. The writing is on the wall. Tough Mom's son is saying, *Fuck you, Mom! You violated my privacy, so I don't respect your rules!*

2. *What would Empowered Mom do?* She might take a deep breath and begin asking questions, such as:

   - How can I help my son better cope with his anxiety and stress?

   - What benefit is he receiving from vaping?

   - Would it be better if I lessen his anxiety somehow rather than punish him and make him feel worse?

   - If I stop stressing about vaping and let it run its course and love my son instead, will he begin to feel better about himself and surrender the need to self-medicate?

The truth is my son tried several prescription medications for anxiety and depression and each had their unpleasant side effects, including aggression and suicidal thoughts. Miles discovered that marijuana effectively calms him. Once I stopped fighting him on his pot smoking and noticed that at least he is not binge drinking or doing heavy illicit drugs, I began to calm down and he did too.

I've always believed that parents are not for leaning upon, but rather exist to make learning unnecessary. ~Dr. Wayne Dyer [1]

Being a mom is tough when we feel the need to hover and be there for our children's every stumble.

Could it be that toddlers cry more in response to mom's frantic reaction to their minor falls than to the pain of the fall itself? I found that as I had more kids, I hovered less and I could more easily overlook every bump and tumble. Kids fall down and carry on when you stand by, observe, and notice. They will come running when they need you.

Could it be that teenagers become more belligerent the more we, as parents, try to push them toward our expectations? *I lovingly release you to the lessons you are here to learn* is a mantra I often found myself saying with each misstep my son made. The line I had to draw was when his actions hurt himself or those around him. Then I had to intervene with professional help or guidance.

Children have an innate sense of who they are. It is disrespectful to negate someone's soul journey or purpose on this planet. Still have boundaries but broaden them for your kids and watch how they expand into the person they are here to be.

Children are like barometers. They seemingly feel Mom even when they don't share the same room. Mom's level of anxiety rises. Before you know it, your child has spilled puzzle pieces and blocks all over the floor and is throwing them at his sister.

Similarly, if Mom feels peaceful, those around her feel it, too, and are more likely to feel calm.

Once I began to truly understand that one of the steps to becoming an Empowered Mom was staying calm even in the midst of chaos, I began to view my kids' disruptive behaviors as learning opportunities.

BUT, there is a huge caveat here. Attempting to be calm when you are experiencing chronic stress and untreated anxiety is like trying to float an inner tube upstream in a rushing river.

As a trained and well-practiced yoga teacher, I set high standards for myself. I tell myself I can handle anything because I have tools like breathing, meditation, and emotional freedom technique (EFT) tapping, a method of controlling anxiety and stress by tapping on various energy points on the body.

So, why was I erupting all the time — daily?

When I learned the devastating effects that chronic, unmanaged stress can have on the body, I began to catch myself when I got triggered.

Is this issue worth losing my peace of mind? I would ask myself.

It took me until 2020 (during quarantine), when I began meditating daily for 20 minutes, that I was able to fully embrace and embody peace as a way of being. Before that, I was too amped up to sit still quietly for more than 10 minutes. I could not fully relax into my being because I was already onto the next thing in my mind.

How could a yoga teacher with 20 years' experience possibly have taken that long to fully live the yogic lifestyle of being calm in the moment, you might ask? I tell students that yoga is a lifelong practice. No one is a master. We are always learning, and the practice truly begins when we leave the mat and enter the world.

They say we teach what we most need to learn. In this case, it took me 20 years. I continue to learn to be more mindfully present and allow the moments to unfold rather than push my agenda through as my Type A, Fiery Volcano self would have it. I can now more mindfully approach things in my task-oriented nature and attend to what is most pertinent.

When the Lava Flow Meets Inner Peace

The Type A achiever in me strives to attain goals. In this pursuit, my actions are forward and aggressive like a volcano. This behavior can become controlling as I blindly seek completion of a task. As I have taught myself to find calm, I have learned to choose a new method to accomplish goals.

These days, I choose three Big Rocks, as introduced in the 5 Steps to Slowing Down in Myth #2, that will move me forward toward my highest aspiration, which is to heal community and facilitate rebirth of connection. We have experienced so much separation recently that many people have forgotten how to deeply connect. Each action I take is imbued with the intention to rebuild a sense of interconnection with the self and society at large.

Each day, I ask that I may be of service to this higher ideal of healing and reconnecting with people. I ask that God reveal to me the three Big Rocks I can take on that day to be of service to this mission.

I can still use the fiery energy of my inner champion to relentlessly pursue a goal but I do it with more presence and intentionality now.

As I learned to merge my achiever self with my free-spirit side, the first big victory was seeing how my steadfast determination to create a happy, harmonious home life would eventually manifest. And you know what? It was way less effort than I could have imagined. I held the intention in my heart and began to live in harmony with life and nature. I opened my eyes more and watched for opportunities.

My resolve to be at peace and at ease became a daily goal. The slower pace of life during quarantine in spring 2020 afforded me the chance to take daily walks where I would meet people who reflected the peace I was attempting to become.

I met a woman named Pamela one day at a local park while both of our dogs were running off leash. I could hear the Canadian accent in her voice as she asked me, "What kind of dog is that?"

"German Shorthaired Pointer," I answered.

"He's beautiful," she gushed.

We continued to talk, and we went on to walk two more of the 1.4-mile loops around the lake. That one walk would become a regular ritual throughout the lockdown.

Pamela is a prayer warrior. Over the course of our many walks, I shared my story and my struggles with her. She would then say the most wonderful prayers inciting the safety and recovery of my son and our relationship. I know her prayers and the connection we shared during those warm spring and summer months contributed to my family peace mission.

If I hadn't taken the time to slow down and be aware of opportunities to connect, I might not have developed a friendship with Pamela.

While I experience longer bouts of peace now, there are still days when I rest in the dark pit of my inner critic. But I now judge myself less harshly for this failing. In the law of attraction circles (thoughts and feelings create your reality) I had been a part of through the years, I had grown averse to feeling depressed for fear of attracting bad things into my life. I now understand knowing that feeling is healing and feelings must be honored, not scorned.

My practice now is to embrace my doubt, fear, anger, and worry like a small child who is hurting, which has made a tremendous difference in my ability to enter into the power of the pause.

The Power of the Pause

Busyness is an addiction, and being busy all the time steals the opportunity to feel the power of the moment. How often do you tend to your task list only to realize later that none of your actions had a long-lasting, sustainable impact? The power of the pause is stepping away from frantic daily activity to discern whether your actions align with your deeper purpose in life.

For me, writing this book had to rise to the top of my priorities. While it is not currently an income-producing activity, it is clearing my body, mind, and soul of subconscious patterns that have been limiting my impact in the world. When I began writing, the title of this book was "I Am *Not* a Supermom." It was through the process of writing and reading my own story that I now claim that I am a Supermom. I accept that the journey has not been what I had envisioned when I held tiny infants in my arms. I am a Supermom because I have embraced my children's uniqueness and will continue to encourage their growth as a unique individual in the world. Empowered now with the belief that everything is here to help me, I now stop shaming and blaming myself and celebrate the learning opportunities and shattering of limiting beliefs my experiences as a mother have given me.

At first, I made myself wrong for not working a traditional full-time job that provides adequate income and security for my family. But then I realized that I am not my bank account or my possessions. I am a pure light shining a message of hope for moms everywhere in the world.

My wish for you, Mom, is that you will experience the power of the pause many times daily.

I know some days you feel like you can't catch your breath. But when you begin to consciously breathe more often, your days become a living meditation. Your breath guides you with present moment awareness to the opportunities that yield to effortless ease in daily life.

Make a note to yourself: When things become difficult, step away. Avoid the path of resistance. When you are breastfeeding your baby, are you checking your social media feed? This is an ideal time to just tune into that precious babe in your arms. Listen to the sounds of her suckling. What wouldn't I give to just feel that pull at my breast just one more time?

When your toddler is throwing a tantrum, ask first, *Are all his needs being met? Is he tired? Hungry? Overstimulated?* Pause. Reflect on the day. When you are running from the grocery to the bank and then to a play date, it is easy to overlook the fact that your child is tired or maybe you forgot to feed him lunch. Instead of scolding him, hug him and find out what he needs.

Sometimes, you have to try different solutions to calm a stressful parenting situation. I used to cry from the frustration I felt hearing my screaming toddler daughter. Nothing I could do or say seemed to calm her down. We would try blowing bubbles or feathers as a distraction, but she would hurl them across the room. I would create a secret hideaway for her to go be quiet. She liked this idea and still does to this day. As a teenager, she relishes her bedroom as a safe, peaceful refuge.

My daughter was chronically overstimulated. As a 4-year-old, a pediatrician would diagnose her with sensory processing disorder. But prior to that, I just thought I had no tolerance, especially because I was suffering from postpartum depression. What a perfect storm!

Even when I would pause, I felt like I was resting in the pit of the volcano. I could not physically relax so I generally kept the kids and me busy all the time.

What if I had just learned to rest more and do less? I am an obstinate learner, and it would take me another nine years to fully embrace the power of the pause. It was like rolling a rock up a mountain. I would make forward progress, and then the rock would roll back over me and so on. Now I am standing at the mountaintop enjoying the power of presence most days. I recognize when I am starting to veer off course and I quickly self correct rather than steamroll through in the name of mindlessly completing another task.

The Power of Presence

In present moment awareness, I open up a powerful portal where the Universe can enter in and empower me to do the unimaginable. I meditate, play my drum or take a play break with my kids to clear my head of doubts that may limit my full expression. Books and coaches and research might provide information. At the end of the day, though, the answers lie within.

My inner wisdom might guide me to a particular book or resource for the answer. And usually, my inner guidance makes absolutely no sense. I love the nonsensical. Laughter and play lead to far greater conclusions than poring over articles and research for the answers. That's the way I choose now. I used to analyze and assess painstakingly, but now I tend to lead more from the heart.

The hardest thing is to accept that the way I flow does not generally match societal standards.

Don't let a mad world tell you that success is anything other than a successful present moment. ~ Eckhart Tolle

The Power of Peace

Peace flows like a river. I love sitting by a mountain stream and feeling the gentle power of flowing water. Albeit, soft and malleable, water can carve rocks over time. While peace may not have as immediate an impact as applying force or, for example, sandblasting a rock to carve a pattern, the effects are more elegant and sustainable when we find the strength from within to implement change. Peace doesn't look very powerful until you reflect on great leaders like Mahatma Gandhi and Martin Luther King Jr. Peaceful resistance means that we corral our inner peace and swallow up the anger of the oppressor and forgive ourselves for making their reality our own.

What does all that mean?

When I am at peace and ease in my own inner sphere, I can allow my children to have their experiences without needing to intervene or fix the situation for them. I praise even the shortcomings and mistakes.

Now, I wish I had celebrated my son's willingness to step out into the world at the age of 15 and go beyond the parameters I had set for him.

Instead of punishing him for disappearing for two days, I could have expressed appreciation after sharing how worried and concerned I had been. I could have said, "I appreciate your independent spirit and desire to explore downtown Denver on your own, but did you consider my feelings when you didn't come home the last two nights?"

That would have felt a lot better than, "Where the hell have you been? I was worried sick, and I filed a runaway report. You can't see your girlfriend anymore!"

Unfortunately, when that incident happened, I was still playing the role of Tough Mom, and I put up higher walls between my son and me.

Luckily, for my younger two, I will approach their teen years from a perspective of learning from them and asking more questions.

The power of peace prevails because I love myself too much to allow stress, anxiety, fear of the unknown, and tension to lead the way. The power of peace allows the present moment awareness in my breath or the sunset or the gentle breeze to override the frantic list of things that society tells me I should do.

Feeling Like a Farce

I am no stranger to being called a Pollyanna or being told I am out of touch with reality.

My stress levels are extremely high as a single mom, presently going through global pandemic times with three kids and a waning income. And yet I keep persisting even when I hear the voice of doubt in myself and others.

As I write, I revisit the pain from the past, and I breathe. At times, it can be challenging to relax. I consider myself relatively healthy and grounded, but I still come unglued from time to time.

I continue to struggle with sleep issues, and friends express concern for my erratic behavior.

"Fake it till you make it," as so many experts advise.

I would change that to: Have compassion for yourself. Acknowledge the small successes each day, and recognize that you are a work in progress.

From one perspective, being a mom is tough these days. There is plenty of evidence to validate that statement. What if you start saying, "Being a mom is simple," or, "Being a mom is easy"? I would much rather seek proof for those declarations.

Here is my proof. When I am peaceful and at ease, I do not need to heal, fix, or change my kids to fit my ideals. They each do their own thing, whether it is to go for a drive with friends or build a tower out of yoga blocks and knock them down or sit in their rooms chatting with friends online. As I have found flow and harmony in my life by doing less and being more present, we are no longer visited by the cops, and the crying, screaming tantrums are now joyful games of Uno Attack around the kitchen table.

Being a mom can be easy when you choose ease. When it gets tough, let that be a signal to pause and experience the power of peace.

Chapter Four

Myth #4: Being a Mom Is Exhausting

Myth-buster: Being a mom can be exhilarating when you use your energy wisely and elicit help from others.

Reality: Setting healthy boundaries is key to managing your energy. Learning to say 'no' leads to freedom.

I would like to begin this chapter with a disclaimer. If you are the mother of an infant, then, yes being a new mom can be exhausting. That is why in many countries in Europe, women take a year off to focus on caring for their babies. The first year, when you are yanked nightly from your sleep by a screaming infant, is taxing. Unfortunately, 6 to 12 weeks is the norm for maternity leave in the United States. It is insane to think we can be thrown back into the workforce while still waking up multiple times a night with an infant and not be exhausted.

With that said, I encourage new moms to ASK FOR HELP. If your family lives elsewhere, ask your neighbors or friends (including church friends) to help you. You can even post a message on your neighborhood association's online board asking for a mother's helper to assist around the house.

For a long time, I was stubborn and never asked for help. As a result, I suffered from postpartum depression, chronic back pain, and insomnia. I was still teaching a pretty full load of fitness classes and being a badass mom. Truth be told, I was fried at the end of every day, and I had no patience for any sort of crying baby or tantrum-throwing toddler.

I was a monster Mom with an unregulated nervous system. But I still practiced or taught yoga most days. You know what? It *is* possible to zone out and detach when doing yoga.

Living in a chronic state of exhaustion might look something like this:

6 a.m.   Wake up feeling exhausted.

6:15 a.m. Stumble to the coffee machine. Start ingesting lots of caffeine.

11 a.m.   Hit a wall and order a latte at the coffee house.

2 p.m.   Is it nap time yet?

5 p.m.   Happy hour and wine to wind down for the day

9 p.m.   Sleeping pills and start the cycle all over again.

I still have my struggles with sleep, although it has gotten much better through the years. I used to go for days sometimes without sleeping, and that was even when I was receiving regular Reiki and acupuncture sessions for sleep management.

I accept that many nights I will awaken around 2 a.m., practice yoga for 30 minutes, and then return to bed for another three hours. I know there is plenty of research to prove the necessity of seven to nine hours of sleep per night for optimal health. I also know that some of the greatest geniuses like Thomas Edison got by on four to five hours of sleep, which he supplemented with power naps.

The Power Nap

As a kindergartner, I attended the morning class. Then I would come home and eat lunch with my mom. Afterward, she would carry me upstairs to her bedroom where we would read a story and then have "nap time." Usually, that meant I would wait to hear my mom's cute little snore then proceed to have playtime on my own.

My mom understood the power of the pause and that nap time is an important rejuvenator. She was also the wise one who advised me to lie down when the baby was napping. Afternoon rest time became survival for my mother. For me, my kids' nap time was the time to start checking off the items on the to-do list.

At least until I became a single mom.

Now, I regularly lie down and listen to a guided meditation at 2 p.m. I fall asleep if my body needs more rest.

When I pause, I can step away from being busy, get quiet, and ask:

- Am I following my soul purpose today?
- Am I contributing in a way that serves the highest and best for all?

When I rest, I can get out of the chaos and observe the day from a more objective place. If I answer *no* to these questions, then I get a chance to reboot and fulfill my purpose. I can state my intention. *I desire a happy, harmonious home.* Then, I will ask a question, *What is the next best step to achieve that goal?* All I have to know is the next step. And that next step may be to thank my kids for being resilient and patient instead of noticing they didn't clean their rooms again.

Changing Our Perspective

If you tell yourself that being a mom is exhausting, you will find verification to prove it. And you might even find yourself taking on more than you need to or committing to activities that don't juice you up.

And this goes back to the busy badge of honor fallacy.

In 2017, a Pew Research survey of American adults found that 77% of American women felt pressure to be an involved parent (compared to 49% of men).[1] Women feel pressure to perform at the highest level as a parent. While, for the most part, the financial burden falls on men in a marriage, single moms still account for 25% of households where the burden of financial support falls solely on her.

I can speak from the perspective of being a single mom who endeavors to be an involved parent while maintaining peace at home and earning enough money to keep everyone happy and healthy.

When I became a solo parent, I had to let go of a lot of previous obligations. I gave up my role as president of a committee at school. I gave up cleaning my home weekly. I let go of the need to enroll my kids in extracurricular activities. I let go of teaching evening classes.

My sole focus had to be on taking care of me and the kids. And that has not been an easy task because the fighter and champion in me will always push to get the job done no matter what.

From Exhaustion to Exhilaration

When I was 26, I helped open a new community wellness center. In the weeks leading up to the grand opening, I sometimes arrived at my office at 5 a.m. ready to go and full of ideas. I effortlessly worked 60-hour weeks. I felt exhilarated and light.

Think back to a project or a time when you felt at ease, highly motivated, and lit up!

What were you doing?

How did you start each day?

What was your attitude?

Write about a time when you were enthusiastic about a project. Answer these questions in a journal or notebook and notice how your awareness of where your motivation comes from can feed your current situation.

Am I suggesting that you can just flip a switch in your head, say, *Being a Mom is exhilarating*, and all of a sudden you will feel electrified?

Not at all.

I know you have lots to do, Mom, especially if you home-school your kids.

Start assessing your energy drains and only do what contributes to your overall worth and value.

1. Eliminate unnecessary chores. What do you currently do that is unnecessary? Do you have to clean the bathroom more than once a week? What is absolutely essential?

2. Delegate tasks. Make a list of tasks you can assign to your kids. I always remind myself that pioneer children worked the farm from a very young age. Our kids can do way more than we give them credit for.

3. Be okay with imperfection. Not every task will be performed to your standards. For instance, your kids likely will not clean as thoroughly as you do.

4. Be okay with good enough and wait for the energy surge to deep clean.

5. Hire some help or look for volunteers. Look for sources of help. Be creative. For a while, some missionaries assisted me with yard work, and they were so gracious to help me.

Being a Mom Is a Dream Come True

Giving birth is one of life's most awesome experiences. As a child, I dreamed of being a mom. I carried my baby dolls with me everywhere I went. I vowed to myself that I would never be one of those working moms who put her kids in daycare.

Bringing my firstborn to daycare for the first time was heartbreaking. It felt so wrong to hand my baby over to someone else. Shortly after I returned to my fitness director job, the club I was working at shut down. My childhood dream of being a stay-at-home mom came true.

I would be one of those moms who took stroller walks in the middle of the day, went to the museum and the zoo, and enjoyed playdates. I found that taking walks while my infant son screamed was draining. Going to playdates with kids of all ages screaming and tearing through the house wore on my nerves. Being a mom was exhausting.

What if I had set my agenda aside, and embraced the awe and wonder of each stage of my child's growth?

Instead, I took those daily walks or runs and pushed through the crying spells. I forced myself to go to the playdates because that's what all the good moms did.

I quickly realized being a stay-at-home mom was not for me. I got a gig at a gym where I worked from 5 a.m. to 9 a.m. every day. Often, I would keep myself awake after the 3 a.m. feeding. I was a sleep-deprived mess, but at least I was bringing home a paycheck and doing my thing.

Now, as an older, more experienced mother, I see ways where I could have done things differently. Instead of pushing through problems, I could have paused. For instance, I could have asked myself, *Why is my son crying when I take him on a walk? What would make my baby happy?*

From the very beginning, I would have approached motherhood as an adventure. An adventure is an exploration into unknown territory.

My five-month trip to Thailand in 2001 was a big adventure. While traveling, I found myself posing questions like, *I wonder where this road leads? What is the history of this Buddhist temple?*

I felt exhilarated most of the time during my travels. I encountered challenges, but I was open to the idea of adventure, and I relied on guides and fellow travelers to steer my way.

Years later, what if I could have approached parenting as a big adventure? Finding solutions to problems could have been an investigation. Not knowing how I would guide or discipline my kids would have become a process of self discovery rather than another opportunity to scorn or shame myself for doing it all wrong. I would have relied more on myself as a resource just as I did that day in Thailand when I got on the wrong bus and ended up in an area of Bangkok where no one spoke English. Eventually I found my way and it was an adventure.

As a younger mom, I was terrified of getting it all wrong, and nothing was going to stop me from getting my body back, not even a wailing baby.

Call it selfishness -- or naivete. What I was doing was not loving to myself. I was exhausted and depleted and probably a terror to live with.

Mom, please do not misconstrue my statement, "A good mom puts herself first to be more for her kids." My actions were not loving. They were self-annihilating. When a behavior exhausts you, it is time to evaluate the value of your actions.

In retrospect, I would have done myself and my son a greater service by slowing down. But I thought that there was no way I could have done that and continued my trajectory toward success.

How to Live an Exhilarating Life

Live as though life is a big adventure. Even the most carefully planned life will offer you unexpected twists and turns. I used to get so frustrated when a stumbling block would get in my way. My approach was to kick that obstacle right out of my path.

When I ruminate about how my son could have possibly dropped out of school, I become frustrated and exhausted. Instead, I can say, "I can't wait to see the path that Miles chooses for himself." I celebrate that he is researching community colleges and learning about the stock market rather than dwelling on the fact that he still vapes in the house and leaves dishes in the sink.

When motherhood is a big adventure, we can take the bumps in the road with greater ease. Life is a cosmic roller coaster. We can look down at the "oh, shit!" or we can rise high to the butterflies-in-the-tummy adventure. Let's enjoy the ride, Moms.

Chapter Five

Myth #5: Moms Do It All

Myth-buster: The more you allow things to happen, the less you fight to control it.

Reality: When you relinquish control and let go of expectations, you will find that there is less to do.

It was the middle of the school day, and a familiar number popped up on my caller ID. It was Deputy Dave.

Now what? I thought.

My son had been caught stealing, pushing a vending machine over at school, smoking dope under a bridge, and then fleeing the cops on foot across the interstate.

Deputy Dave's phone calls always seemed to come right in the middle of a business conversation, and I knew that answering the call would instantly slow any momentum I had gained in my workday.

I picked up the phone. "Hello, Deputy Dave, is everything okay?"

"We have Miles here, and another officer is bringing him to the JAC [juvenile assessment center]," he informed me.

"What happened?" I asked. This is a question I would ask ad nauseum.

"He stole a sandwich from Walmart,"

At the end of my rope, I said, "His father will be picking him up this time. Call him."

And just like that, I passed the accountability stick back to his dad, even though I knew my former spouse had verbally and physically abused our son in the past.

I felt there was something that the two of them needed to work out that only they could resolve. I had exhausted *all* of my resources, and I was going crazy. I was likely fired from my job that September because the drama of my situation kept spilling over into my daily life.

Further, I could no longer subject my younger two children to the frequent disruptions and volatile arguments that were the norm during this time in our lives.

Sometimes, Moms, you have to surrender and let go and watch everything fall apart to rebuild again.

This story didn't end well. After two months of living with his father, my son continued his antics of sneaking out and coming home after curfew.

His father, however, has a much shorter fuse than I do.

I saw the video that Miles took that evening. His father had pinned him to the ground, elbow on neck and shouting obscenities, telling our son he was worthless.

Miles ended up on my living room couch that night. The markings on his throat prompted me to call Child Protective Services, the fourth case I had filed in three years. This one would again get dropped.

Moms, I was greatly disappointed in the *system*. Realizing I could no longer do it all, I asked for help from the Department of Human Services, and ended up feeling a fool time and time again.

An abuser can turn up the charm in an interview. A narcissist can paint the prettiest of pictures and manipulate anyone, even a trained psychologist. Time after time, my former spouse beat the system, and I began to side with my son.

It was Thanksgiving week 2019 when my son returned to me downcast and abused. He didn't even want to attend a Thanksgiving celebration with me. Instead, he stayed home in bed all day.

Would a good mom have stayed home with her distraught child? I still ask myself today.

I opted to go to my friend's Thanksgiving Day gathering. When I came home and saw how worn down my son was, I knew something much worse was going on.

His throat was swollen to the point he could barely breathe. At the doctor's office, as I awaited the results from the endoscopy procedure and X-rays, I secretly hoped that trauma would be revealed and finally there would be evidence to charge his father with abuse.

It turned out my son had mono.

He had already lost the first semester of his junior year, so he spent three weeks in bed recovering from mono and basically failing all of his classes. I lowered all standards and just focused on my son's recovery.

While his physical health did bounce back, his psyche was deeply damaged.

Depression had a grip on him, and his anger could quickly flare to rage. His depression made it difficult for him to focus, and he would sleep most days past noon.

I enrolled him in online school just three months before the rest of the world went into lockdown when all students would begin attending school remotely.

Online school requires a lot of discipline. My son did not even have it in him to log in. I would receive phone calls from the school indicating he wasn't logging in and that he was falling behind.

My daily prompts to get up and get going with school were met with frustrated resistance. In Miles' mind, he had figured out the minimum he needed to do to pass. Unfortunately, he had fallen so far behind, catching up was impossible.

At a certain point, I honored my son's request for me to stop prodding him to attend school.

As a mom, I had to realize that I couldn't do it for him. Mom could not do it all. I had to watch him fail.

He lost an entire year of school and would enter into his senior year with earned credits equivalent to a high school sophomore.

Learning to Let Go

Moms, when you decide you can no longer do it all, it means you will spend less time nagging, pushing, and finding ways to make other people change to meet your expectations.

Every parent expects their kids to graduate high school. We all want at least that for our kids.

My kid could not fit into the school system. His failing grades did not reflect the bright, mature thinker he could be.

And yet, when he passed four GED practice tests, I could not dispute that he had somehow gained the knowledge he needs to successfully enter community college to pursue his passion for counseling and learning about the effect of childhood trauma on the brain.

My next step in letting go is trusting that my 17-year-old will successfully complete his GED tests and enroll in community college.

He still sleeps until noon most days, and he waits until the very last minute to do everything. I can't do it for him, and he may have to fail a few more times before he gets it.

Yet, he seems to have it figured out. He found a community college with a specialty program that focuses on adolescent trauma and abuse. He plans to get his driver's license when he is 18; no permit or class is required.

I will wait, watch, guide, and remind, but I no longer make phone calls for him or call to make sure he's followed through on his appointments.

To raise an adult, we must be willing to stop doing it all for our kids.

And you know what? It is still not easy for me to let go and watch my kids fall short.

But, I must remind myself that Miles is falling short of *my* standards. The bar he has set for himself may be much lower than his overachieving mom might set, but I must love, honor, and respect my son.

When Mom does it all, she looks for evidence that everyone else is making her load heavier. Her busy schedule causes her to let her mental, physical, and emotional health slide. The chaos of her life is evidence to her that she needs to do more to fix it, and eventually, she burns out.

This life is like racing an Indy car to the checkered flag while running on fumes. You will be bound to sputter and spin out, Mom, before you reach the finish line. If you continue to ignore the rattling and shaking of your body, something eventually will come along to show you that you cannot do it all.

As a young mom, I had it all together. I would put one or both of my kids in the bike trailer and ride to work at the downtown athletic club where I worked as a personal trainer.

One day, I was teaching my Platinum Club fitness class when the studio floor started spinning out from underneath me. Within minutes, two of my 70-year-old class participants were holding me up on either side, guiding me to a chair. My toddler son was in the child watch while I was being taken off in a stretcher to Denver Health Hospital for evaluation.

They checked for brain tumors with a CT scan. In the end, I was diagnosed with vertigo. This was the beginning of a long period of realizing that I cannot do everything. I spent the next several days in bed with my head spinning, as I took a break from being a traditional Supermom.

For years to come, my vertigo symptoms would be an early indicator to me that I had to lighten my load. Never again did I want to experience being led out of my workplace on a stretcher while concerned coworkers and clients looked on. Never again did I want to feel like I was falling through a sinkhole to my own demise.

I would still struggle to ask for help. I would be repeatedly tested as the load increased with the birth of two more kids.

When my daughter was born in 2007, I experienced a huge test in patience and letting go. Vienna was colicky. To most parents, hearing that word is akin to receiving a jail sentence.

From October 2007 through January 2008, my life consisted mostly of cleaning up spit up, rocking and bouncing my baby, and generally feeling frustrated that my life had been interrupted by all this intense daily crying.

Vienna would cry eight to 12 hours a day, and everything I did was aimed at getting her to calm down. I spent hours each day with her in my arms as I bounced on the fit ball. Getting my son to preschool each morning was a feat in itself. Even though the school was only one mile away, enduring the crying while going through the frustratingly slow process of getting everyone into the car would break me every day.

What if I had asked one of the parents in the neighborhood to pick up my son?

I didn't want to be a burden on anyone, so I reserved those requests for only the most desperate of times.

As my house became a wreck due to my daily role as chief executive soother, I employed the use of a Baby Bjorn. With this front baby carrier, I could wear my baby and get it all done. Baby-wearing was all the rage, in line with the attachment parenting trend of the day. I was conquering this colic problem!

My back would tell a different story. A word of caution to moms of babies: Your body needs time to heal, and even though baby carriers are convenient, they encourage moms to do too much too soon. Hell, I remember cooking stir-fry with my baby on my chest. Sounds real safe, right?

But at least I was feeding my family a fresh-cooked meal, just like a good mom, I thought at the time.

Pushing Too Hard

Those three months spent mothering and soothing my colicky baby girl took its toll on my nervous system.

But I literally bounced right back into teaching and training once my daughter was old enough for daycare. I began teaching the new fitness craze that had arrived at my workplace -- the Kangoo Jump, crazy shoes that looked like ski boots with springs on them. I immediately volunteered to do the training and start teaching these bouncy, jumping classes. Let's just say, it did a number on my weak and recently traumatized pelvic floor. And by the way, you are not supposed to wet your pants when you jump, Moms.

A month later, the club would introduce a new Pilates chair to the class schedule. I was excited when the club selected me as one of the instructors to take the training. My daughter was four months old. My pelvis felt like it was shearing and separating during some of the exercises, but I kept going. I pumped breast milk on breaks during the three-day training and amazed the other instructors with my Supermom capabilities.

A few months after undertaking my full class teaching schedule, I found myself making weekly trips down to the physical therapy clinic at my workplace for heat packs and therapy just so I could get through my workday. I suffered from severe back pain. I had no idea that the culprit was my insanely active schedule.

I'm sure that teaching as many as three fitness classes several days per week while pregnant with my daughter had no bearing on the breakdown of my back and the rest of my body. I felt like I was such a great model of how to be a Supermom. Work out hard while pregnant. Yeah! What a badass I was!

Bending Toward Restoration

It was May 2009. My daughter was 18 months old, my son was not quite 6, and my back felt like an 80-year-old's. For Mother's Day, I treated myself to a special three-hour restorative yoga class. I had never been to this type of yoga class, and I knew I needed it.

When I arrived, the room was packed with people, props, and the promise of healing and good feelings. Live harp music made this event extra special.

The instructor advised us that if we felt uncomfortable at any time to ask for help and one of her assistants would guide us to a better position. "Please take care of yourself," she suggested. "Lying here suffering is not being a good student. We are here to help you have a great experience."

During the second pose of the class, I was lying back on a long, rolled-up blanket tube when my back began to spasm. I tried bending my knees. No relief. I rocked from side to side. The pain intensified.

One of the instructors must have observed me trying to fix myself. She placed a hand on my upper chest and abdomen, and asked me to breathe. Whispering in my ear, she asked me what I needed. I told her I could not lie still anymore because my back was aching.

She offered me an extra bolster and a blanket to boost me up. I felt so nurtured and supported. As a mother and in my work, I spent my days nurturing others. What a novel experience to be cared for by someone else.

That class may have been the first time I had completely let myself be taken care of in the six years since I had become a mother. The harp music lulled me into a peaceful place, and my back finally found relief. As I transitioned from pose to pose, the teacher/angel was right there to support me getting into the next pose in the sequence.

When the class ended, the instructor advised us to move slowly. "There is absolutely no rush," she told us. "You probably don't feel like you can drive right away. Stick around. Have a cup of tea and get grounded."

I took full advantage of this offer and continued to enjoy my kid-free afternoon to the fullest.

I sang my praises for the class to the instructor, who also owned the studio.

"I am offering a 100-hour Restorative Yoga Teacher Training starting in October," she told me.

"How do I sign up?" I immediately responded. I spent the next several months attending classes and preparing myself for what would become one of the most life-changing nine months of my life.

Instructor training began on October 9, 2009. That same day, I also had a doctor's appointment. At that appointment, I would find out that I was pregnant and due June 16. This was a complete and utter surprise.

From the doctor's office, I drove to my first instructor training. Fortuitously, the training would extend throughout the rest of my pregnancy. Each month until June, I would spend a three-day weekend in my instructor-training class, finally teaching my body and mind to relax.

It turned out that restorative yoga was the missing piece in my health regime and the lifeline that started to help me discover that I cannot do it all. Resting and relaxing were difficult for me at first. My body resisted relaxing. As I let myself go deeper into these practices, I discovered the peace that lies within me.

My son, Ian, was born a week late on June 23, and it was the most peaceful and graceful birth of my three children. His disposition was calm and easygoing. After my colic trauma, I was relieved to now have an infant who could go with the flow.

That began the formation of a theory. What if all the jumping around and busyness of my daughter's pregnancy had affected the development of her nervous system? I spent a lot of time practicing restorative yoga during Ian's pregnancy, and he turned out relatively calm as a baby.

All this is theory, but when I discovered epigenetics -- the study of the way genes express themselves based on behaviors and environmental factors. Epigenetics, thus, does not change the DNA sequence but it alters its expression. Could my busy lifestyle with little time for rest be influencing my children and their development? I theorized that my daughter's colic may have been due to my overstimulated nervous system brought on by my relentless schedule during that pregnancy when I would teach as many as 3 exercise classes in a day. Contrast that with my peaceful pregnancy with my youngest son where restorative yoga was the cornerstone of each day. He was such a calm and well adjusted infant in comparison to his sister. I wondered if I was onto something.

When Mom is stressed in pregnancy, her body produces a hormonal cocktail that the baby ingests, too. Mom is stressed. Baby is stressed, too. Mom is calm. Baby is calm, too.

Many people complimented me on my physique and how quickly I had bounced back after my pregnancies. I didn't do my body any favors by doing too much too soon. Restorative yoga teacher training during my pregnancy taught me that slowing down and recovery are vital to overall fitness.

I still packed my schedule full after my third child was born, but at least I had an awareness of what being relaxed felt like in my body.

Trying to Do It All

It was the summer after the birth of my third child. My older son was home from school, and I dropped my daughter's daycare to save money. My husband's mother was battling terminal cancer, and he was emotionally unavailable.

It was my goal and duty to still be everything and more for my kids. Two weeks postpartum, I took Miles to tennis lessons and then to the pool for swimming lessons. Nothing was going to slow me down -- until I got the diagnosis.

At my six-week postpartum visit, my doctor said my mental health evaluation indicated I had postpartum depression. I was wondering why I was flying off the handle, screaming at my kids every day.

At the same time, my 3-year-old daughter had daily scream-ing tantrums. She was inconsolable. This was two years before we found out she had sensory processing disorder. I still wonder whether her sensitive little nervous system was so innately wired to mine that she felt all my stress and anxiety.

I had absolutely no time to calm down and slow down. Even my own yoga practice was usually geared toward planning the sequence for my next class.

Added to the mix, my infant son was in and out of the hospital with what would be diagnosed as asthma by the time he was 14 months old. We spent several nights in breathing tents at the hospital. Have you ever tried to contain a toddler inside one of those things?

The weight of these hospital stays fell on me because I was still nursing and my husband had to keep working.

Again, I wonder if my anxious nature -- and thus my inability to slow down and breathe -- influenced my son and his sensitive respiration.

Let me be clear, I am in no way blaming myself for children's health challenges. I just wonder if they would have learned to better self-regulate if I had dropped all the doing and been there more for them by slowing down.

Final Straw

If there was ever a time that taught me that mom can't do it all, it was moving day, March 22, 2012. The day before, my toddler son had been admitted to the hospital with yet another breathing episode. The doctor sent him home with an oxygen tank, and our tiny 900-square-foot home was covered in boxes waiting to be filled. My sister-in-law came over to help us pack but having the whole house packed by 7 p.m. on moving day was looking unattainable.

Imagine a living room packed full of boxes, and a toddler with 50 feet of plastic tubing attached to an oxygen tank ambling all around. The day was spent unwrapping him from the mess.

At one point, I surrendered. I put my toddler in a stroller and headed off to let the others do the packing. Even then, I was talking to our lender who said he couldn't have our closing papers for our new house ready for at least a week. We would eventually end up living in a hotel for a week with our three kids under the age of 8.

While you might think that this moving episode would have brought me to my knees with the realization that I cannot do it all, what really forced the final surrender was the breakup of my marriage in 2016.

After I filed for divorce, my oldest brother had these words of advice for me: "Gina," he said, "The number-one thing you have to do is take care of yourself. Eat the best foods. Exercise. Be clear in your head. You are going to need all your strength to get through this."

I was so stressed and anxious that eating healthy wasn't even an option. I pretty much stopped eating and quickly dropped 20 pounds.

My friends began bringing me food as I wasted away. I learned to ask for help, and I received it. I accepted offers to clean my home. I gratefully accepted the home-cooked meals that friends delivered.

There is nothing pretty about divorce. I truly felt that I was acting in the best interest of my family. However, my former spouse was hurt deeply, and as the saying goes, *Hurt people, hurt people.*

I knew that the daily doses of arguing and observing more discord than harmony was not healthy for my kids. What I did not anticipate were the years of unraveling and restructuring that it has taken to find our new normal. One thing that became quickly apparent was that daily home-cooked meals and a sparkling clean home were two things I would have to sacrifice in favor of taking care of myself.

I still question how I was able to keep all four of us afloat, especially when I was earning little to no income in the early stages. I accepted government assistance, charitable contributions, and a whole lot of grace from God.

I did the best I could with the tools I had available to me. I had taken a co-parenting class as required by the courts. In that class I learned that, "Neither parent shall speak or write derogatory remarks about the other parent to the child, or engage in abusive, coarse or foul language, which can be overheard by the child whether or not the language involves the other parent."

When my former spouse wrote a text to our son, "Your mom doesn't care about you kids. She is only focused on herself and what she wants," did that have a negative impact on him? I think so, and as a result, my parenting role had been undermined and my ability to do it all was negatively affected.

As I watched the pieces of my family literally begin to fall apart and my relationship with my kids deteriorate, my motivation to keep up with chores dissipated.

My weeks sometimes involved three hours of sessions with therapists for my kids and me. My business, fledgling at that point, took an extreme nosedive in progress as I struggled just to keep my head above water each day.

Mainstays throughout this time period were daily exercise and mindfulness practices that kept me going physically, mentally, and emotionally.

If I taught my kids one thing through this long journey it is that even when we are going through stressful times, we must keep self-care at the forefront of our priorities.

Now, in 2021, with the pandemic still inflicting a good dose of trauma upon our world in lockdown, I see so many people keeping busy, but health and well-being are priorities for only a minority of people.

Being in constant fight-or-flight mode drains our energy. When people who are otherwise sedentary tell me they have no time or energy for exercise, I translate that to mean that they have an overstimulated nervous system. We could also call this burnout.

How to Prevent Burnout

Does having an immaculate home make you a good mom?

Does having a schedule full of carpools and extracurricular activities make you a better mom?

Do you put everyone else's needs (including the dog's) before yourself?

Having a perfectly tidy home, children actively involved in activities all the time and having all your ducks in a row might be an outward expression of your mad mothering skills. I would further question at what cost you are producing these results. If you feel exhausted, anxious, depressed, you tend to isolate yourself and you are unable to concentrate, you may be experiencing burnout.

In my wellness coaching business, the two most frequent objections I hear to hiring me for service are (1) I can't afford that or it's not in my budget; and (2) I have too many balls in the air right now.

Do you budget for self-care, Mom? (And I don't mean manicures and coffee.) Do you spend more monthly on one child's activities than you do on your own self-actualization? If you have a steady source of income, it's okay to take out a loan or a line of credit for coaching or other services that support your well-being. The return on investment is typically much larger than the initial upfront investment.

You say you have too many balls in the air? It never slows down, Mom, until you decide to make the commitment to yourself. When you prioritize self-care, balls that once seemed so important fall to the ground, and eventually, your life becomes more manageable because you are in better control of yourself.

When I was going through my son's repeated runaways in 2019, as I stated before, I hired a high-performance coach who taught me how to calm down in those tumultuous times. I had a ton of balls in the air, tracking my son's whereabouts, running my business, putting my best self into my work even though I was operating on three or four hours of sleep.

My financial resources were limited as I was just trying to keep my family in survival mode. I did not budget for coaching. But I knew that if I invested in myself, I would acquire the necessary tools to manage my high-stress existence with grace and ease, and then the money would start to flow.

I was right. In the first month, I hit a record number of sales for the medical-device company I represent and I picked up a new private client. The $2,000 investment I made in myself yielded a $7,000 return. Not bad.

My point in sharing this story is to help squash some limiting beliefs that you may hold that are preventing you from being even more of who you are. These might include: (1) I have to pay for all my kids' stuff before my own; and (2) it is irresponsible to go into debt for unplanned expenses (especially on myself).

When your kids see you becoming healthier and happier and more at peace with yourself, they will ask for less.

It's true.

I think, at this point, my kids would rather that I invest in myself because living in a peaceful, harmonious home is far more desirable than having a schedule packed full of activities.

Think back to your own childhood for a moment. Did your mom take you to all the events you wanted? Did your parents force activities upon you?

While it may seem like keeping your kids busy is the right thing to do, ask yourself: Is my child capable of finding activities and opportunities without spending money? If the pandemic and lockdown has taught us one thing, it is that we can become very creative when we have less to do outside the home.

My mother did not appear to experience burnout. As a child, growing up the youngest of 10 kids, I became my mother's right hand. I pushed one grocery cart while she pushed the other. I cooked and cleaned with my mom. I tagged along for my mom's activities. While she played tennis, I hit balls on the backboard or played with my dolls. While she was bowling twice a week, I learned to socialize in the bowling alley child-watch area.

By the time I entered elementary school, sports became a regular thing, and my mom attended every game she could. But her life was never centered on getting us kids to as many activities as possible. In fact, most days, I walked a mile home from school because my mom had other things to do. While I disliked having to walk on those cold and sometimes rainy days, I am sure I am healthier for having done it.

Today, 38% of parents spend five or more hours per week driving their kids.[1] That is a lot of time invested. Stop and ask yourself how you could reduce your drive time. Consider using driving services, such as HopSkipDrive. Also ask yourself how you can integrate physical activity into your busy driving schedule. Increasing your active time each day will undoubtedly stave off symptoms of burnout, too.

Let's say you have five minutes while you wait for your kids to get out of practice. Could you get out of the car and walk or do squats? I know it is so much easier to sit and check your social media feed. Which activity is better for you at the moment? Maybe checking social media is the best use of your time. That is for you to decide.

I would run laps around the soccer field while my son practiced, then kick the soccer ball with my younger son and play on the monkey bars with him to fill the 90-minute practice time. All the other parents planted themselves on the sidelines with their fold-up chairs, phones in hand, tending to very important business.

Lest you think I am judging these parents, I am simply sharing observations.

Lighten the Load, Mom

I look for movement opportunities all day long. Even when I write, I make sure I get up every 30 minutes to move.

When Mom does it all, she rarely looks out for herself. She might feel busy, but busy and staying active are different things. Does your busy schedule make you feel alive or does it drain you? If you love playing carpool mom and soccer mom, then go for it.

I just want to say that in my profession, I have worked with way too many middle-aged women who are having an epiphany now that the kids are older. Chronic health conditions and weight gain have slowed the traditional Supermom way down. She can no longer keep up with the kids who are now teenagers. She might even wonder if she will live to see her grandkids.

Remember the woman who was described as a master multi-tasker who always put her kids first in her obituary? I'm sure her kids would rather have Mom around now as a healthy, vibrant grandmother.

Instead, they just have memories of a mom who put herself out for everyone else to her own demise. Being a soccer champion with no mom to watch the kid compete in college-level games seems contradictory.

How about if we flip the Moms Do It All myth to read; Mom does what she can without sacrificing her own health to be more for her children.

Do less to be more for your kids in the moment, Mom. You are enough when you stay calm and centered in your own heart.

Chapter Six

The New Story

You don't have to play by the old rules, Mom. You don't have to always put your kid's needs first, exhaust yourself multitasking, or try to do it all. You can write a new story, one that honors and supports you while benefiting your whole family. Here's an example from my own life.

It was a Friday afternoon, January 22, 2021, and I came home unexpectedly between appointments. It smelled like Cheech and Chong had taken up residence upstairs. Reluctantly, I poked my head into my son's bedroom. First, I saw the vape pen on the floor.

He looked at me like a deer caught in the headlights.

"Really?" I was disappointed. "Just one day after you sat downstairs in the living room and promised Mike (the Guardian Ad Litem, a court-appointed guardian who watched over my son while he was on probation) that you would write up a solid argument as to why I should allow you to use marijuana.

"You are not only violating my house rules, but you are violating the law, too." With that, I left the house and reported the incident to Mike.

Remember Tough Mom. She would have confiscated the vape pen, chucked it in the trash, screamed at the top of her lungs, and forbidden her son to see his friends.

Instead, Empowered Mom calmly expressed her disillusionment with his behavior and blatant disrespect for her house rules, and proceeded with her day.

Flashback to April 15, 2020. We had been in lockdown for nearly a month, and life at home was strained to say the least.

As I stood at the top of my stairs that morning, head in hands, adrenaline pulsing through my veins, Officer Jones asked me, "What do you want me to do? Since he has been to the JAC three times already, I advise you to send him to Mount View Youth Services Center. Due to COVID, the JAC is closed now anyways."

A half-hour prior to the police's arrival, I had intended to begin my day with yoga. It was 6 a.m.

I eagerly rolled out my mat, but the blaring rap music coming from my son's room next door rattled my nerves.

I knocked on the door and saw he was half asleep.

"Your music is so loud," I complained. "Will you turn it down?"

He mumbled something and turned over.

Figuring he hadn't heard me, I reached for the volume button on his speaker to turn it down.

Out of nowhere, he grabbed my hand.

I then snatched up his prized possession, the high-tech speaker he had purchased after he got his first paycheck.

A moment later, we were in a grappling match, as he desperately tried to pry the speaker from my arms.

I tumbled to the bed, as he held one arm behind my back.

At this point all my fight or flight hormones were raging and I wasn't giving up.

Freed from his straitjacket hold, I raced for the stairs. He got there first and blocked my escape up the stairs.

I grasped his arm to pull it away with all my force. I continued to struggle, but I carefully withdrew to avoid leaving marks on his body.

I surrendered and screamed out for my 9-year-old son.

"Ian!!" I yelled, breathless. "Call 911!"

I opened the basement window and screamed, "HELP!" I was out of my mind in rage. How could this be happening?

I sat in a chair crying, frantically while my oldest kept his post at the bottom of the stairs.

The loud rap at the door came next. Cops never knock lightly. There is always a pound of authority.

Even when the deputies approached the stairs and commanded Miles, "Step away from the stairs!" my son maintained his guard.

Eventually, they handcuffed him and led him into his bedroom while another officer took a report from me.

What was I going to do? Send my son to the slammer? Put him in the same environment with kids who had stolen or possibly attempted murder?

How could I do that?

Officer Jones looked at me and said, "Mrs. Fontaine, I have been coming here for years. I know you don't want to do this, but I think it's time. Or would you rather have his behavior continue?"

I conceded. I wept as I watched my first born be ushered away in handcuffs for his trip to Mount View Youth Services Center.

I tell these two stories to demonstrate how in nine months I was able to change the story and become a parent who flows with ease rather than fights with resistance.

While it may seem like it is our job to force our kids to participate in athletics or youth group at church because we know what is best for our kids, I realize now that my role as a parent of a defiant teen is to allow him to learn from experience and to support him in being the best version of himself. That requires a fair amount of failure.

Reclaim Your Joy

A myth is a story that helps us define who we are as people. Myths give us identity and purpose. Yet there is no way to prove that a myth is true.

Does a good mom really put her kids first or is that a widely held cultural myth? Does being a mom have to be tough and exhausting because we are trapped into the myth that *mom does it all?* Maybe you have been greatly rewarded with the fruits of your efforts and your master multitasking skills. Is your kid the star of his soccer team? Did your daughter get the lead part in the school play? Do you hear athletes praising Mom in their victory speeches after the championship game?

Do the accomplishments and failures of our children reflect our adequacy or inadequacy as a parent? No. Being you, Mom, is enough. It's okay to step away and give your child space to grow and figure out how to overcome challenges. It's okay to let your older child pay his own way to the next soccer tournament instead of funding it for him.

You *can* maintain your identity, pursue your dreams, take care of yourself, *and* be a joyous, energetic mom who inspires her kids just by being strong and resilient.

If the myth that putting your children first and running yourself into the ground to make sure they have every opportunity is working for you, then there is no need to change the story.

I am ready to reclaim myself as a woman who chooses ease, freedom, and joy as my guideposts in life. How about you, Mom?

I have outlined the five myths that no longer need to define us as moms. You don't have to sacrifice yourself to be a good mom. You no longer need to work from dawn to dusk and run yourself to exhaustion to get it all done.

2020 was disastrous for the moms who continued to do it all. We watched all of our expectations and mythical stories of what it means to create a perfect family life explode before our very eyes.

But from the Big Bang, so to speak, comes the evolution of motherhood.

If one thing became very clear to us in 2020, it is that health is our greatest wealth.

Stress is the number one killer of our immune response. Why did so many more people fall victim to the second wave of COVID-19? My theory is that months of quarantine, home-schooling, working, keeping up with the house, the new puppy, and online happy hours took its toll on our nervous systems, and our immune functions became compromised. Add to that the fact that social distancing reduced the demand for our sovereign bodies to do one of their most vital functions -- fight off germs. And with time for the virus to spread, this time, our immune system could not fight it.

Our Supermom egos could not survive the pandemic. My hope for you is that you began to realize that life can be rich and fulfilling without carpooling kids around to activities.

What if we instead decided to shift the myth that moms have to do it all, sacrifice themselves, and work extra hard during these times of unprecedented demand? Some of you have been working from home and navigating rocky relationships all while trying to homeschool your kids and keep everyone healthy and safe from the pandemic. I propose that moms lead by example and begin to reclaim their passion, interests, and wellbeing in order to be even more joyous, fulfilled women. As you take your time back, your kids will push back in the beginning and as they see you find your happy place, they will stop placing demands on your time and energy and enjoy you being YOU.

How to Create a New Story

Here is how we start to change the story.

#1 Accept that life may be messy and disorganized during times of change.

#2 Stay calm and don't judge yourself.

#3 Ask "I wonder how we are going to get through _____ (fill in the blank with your challenge)."

#4 Remain calm and watch for the next step to appear.

#5 Take it slowly one step at a time.

#6 Realize that everything is here to help you discover the love that you are.

#7 Keep going deeper to the place of heart. The TRUTH can only arise when we are at peace.

When we are revved up, we cannot operate from the heart. We fall into those deeply ingrained patterns of being busy. Busy does not equal success. And there is no intrinsic reward for being busy.

Just last night I was reading the elementary school newsletter. There were links to six articles about monitoring internet use with your kids. One article showed a bar graph indicating that more than 60% of parents monitor their kids' website surfing.

I monitored my kids' phone usage for a short period of time but when the Bark app flagged benign texts that seemed profane but were really in fun, I lost my need to screen my kids' texts.

Call me an irresponsible parent, but I certainly do not have the time or inclination to monitor three kids' internet usage.

I accept that their eyes will land on content that is inappropriate the same way I found R-rated movies on HBO when I was 13 years old. I trust that I have raised them with strong values to discern what is helpful and beneficial from what is damaging and unhealthy.

My 10-year-old chooses to find the "clean" versions of his favorite rapper. My daughter might spend most of the time on her phone chatting with friends these days, and I trust that she will eventually get bored of the incessant online stream and seek refuge in her family.

I value privacy. Monitoring my kids' whereabouts on an app and reading their private messages feels like a violation of my trust in them.

My oldest son felt violated when I asked to check his phone. I had good reason to monitor his usage given that he had abused social media in the past. When I finally confiscated his phone, one of his friends gave him an old phone. My son could then surf the web without my oversight.

Let's put ourselves in our kids' shoes with an example from our youth. Did you used to pass notes to your friends in high school? A typical note might have said something like this: What's up? Do you think John really likes me? I saw him watching me at Tina's party last Friday, but I was so wasted.

Just imagine if your mother had asked you to empty all the notes from your purse at the end of your day at high school and she read every single one of them. Horrifying thought, right?

Why, then, do we take it upon ourselves to dip into our tween and teenage kids' private worlds?

I have enough to do as a woman, mother, business owner, dog owner, friend, and daughter. I know one thing, and that is when I am calm and at peace in myself, everyone else around me is, too. (And sometimes, we just have to let the sour apples rot.)

So let's create a new myth -- a new story. Let's call it: I am enough, and my best is good enough. I am choosing the path of ease.

In this story, Mom lets her kids take a more active role in day-to-day activities.

In this new story, Mom puts herself first and says "no" to doing things that do not support her well-being, even when it disappoints her kids.

In this story, Mom focuses fully and completely on one activity or task at a time and allows herself grace to get less done. Her primary goal becomes being more of herself so that she can be a role model of loving self-care. As she begins to let go of perfectionism, incessant carpooling, and committee meetings, she begins to realize her full potential as a unique individual and her kids get on board with this simpler lifestyle because Mom is happier, more settled, and at ease.

On a recent family trip to Florida to visit my parents, my two teenage kids complained about being surrounded by old people. "Can we go to a big city like Miami or Orlando?" they begged.

"No," was my answer. I needed calm and serenity after several weeks of packing and moving. My older two kids spent most of the time on their electronics indoors during that vacation, and I allowed them to have their experience without caving into their will. Did I hear about it every day? Yes. Did I cave in and placate their desire? No. I knew that they likely would have found things to complain about in the big city, too.

I am a joyous mom who takes life as it comes and who takes smaller bites out of the experience of living. And my kids, parents, friends, and former clients may not always like or understand the decisions I make.

Last year, just before Christmas, my 17-year-old son called. "Mom," he said, "I'm at the dog adoption place, and I just got paid. I want to buy a puppy for the family for Christmas."

We already have a pretty vivacious dog, and with the potential of moving in the next year. I simply said, "I love that you are thinking about the family, but I cannot take on having a new puppy right now."

"But I'll take care of it and feed it and walk it and buy him his food. It will be like a fresh start for all of us."

My son has a big heart, and I appreciated his sentiments. "I will listen to your reasons, but ultimately, in the end, I am the adult and I get the final vote," I explained.

He didn't talk to me for days after I denied his request.

And then, just last week, he called me and asked, "Can I get a TV for the family? I just got paid, and I know Vienna and Ian would like it, too."

Again, I had to say no. We are moving soon, and I don't want to add anything new to the house.

He argued, "You NEVER listen to me. You always do what you want, and you don't care what I want."

I can listen to my child and hear his requests and unless there is a compelling argument as to why this would be the best decision for all involved, then I stick with what I know is best for the family.

I would love to indulge all my kids' whims, but when I deny what I know to be best for all of us, I am not respecting myself.

My son's story is, "Mom doesn't care what I want. She is just doing what she wants so she can be happy."

These days, I am still in the fiery, destructive phase of change. I still get triggered, and I still scream out in frustration from time to time, but it is no longer my daily existence. When I am having a disagreement with my oldest son, I am taking it less personally. It helps me to remember that even though he towers over me at 6'2", he is still a kid, and his brain is still developing.

I still ask for the dishes to be put in the dishwasher, and my son continues to do it on his own timeline, not mine. The trick is to let it go and live my life. And if I want it done, then I do it, but don't complain or berate my kid while doing it.

In the book, *Loving What Is*, Byron Katie recalls asking her kids to pick their socks up off the floor. She would nag them daily, but she would always end up begrudgingly picking up the socks anyway. Then one day, she realized that having socks off the floor was really only important to her, so she began to lovingly retrieve the dirty socks and deposit them in the hamper. Soon, her kids stopped leaving socks out on the floor. Could her change in attitude have flipped the switch in her kids from resistance to willingness?

It really is amazing how a mother's internal environment can affect her children even when she tries to keep her crappy day or frustrated anger under wraps. That is why changing the story from Myth #1 *Good Moms Always Put Their Kids' Needs First* is so key to creating the life you want. When you begin to put yourself first, Mom, you will feel guilty at first. You will feel like there is something else you should be doing.

As you step away from the societal standards that tell you things like, *Being a mom is tough or exhausting,* you will begin to feel a lightness that frees you up to run and giggle with your kids more often. Likely, you will catch yourself stepping back into the chaos and filling your plate with way too many obligations. But, once you have the experience of thriving on peace instead of chaos, you will never say things like, *I thrive on chaos.* Peace will become your state of being, and more of the important, potent work you are here to do will be accomplished.

Cynthia, my loving friend and mother of two grown boys, says, "I am who I perceive myself to be."

So guess what?

If you go around saying things like,

"I am so busy,"

"My life is chaos,"

"No one respects me," and

"A mother's work is never done,"

your life will, indeed, reflect back exactly what you declare.

The question, then, to ask yourself is this: *Am I healthy and happy with the way things are?* If your answer is *Yes!* then, by all means, continue to load your plate full with activities and tasks and enjoy.

But if you are tired, exhausted, have early signs of chronic illness, are depressed, or suffer from anxiety, the question to ask is, *What would I rather have instead?*

I might say, *I desire to live in a healthy, harmonious home.*

And I did, in fact, write those very words on a piece of paper at the beginning of 2020. The year began with an uptick in the discord. With each confrontation with my son and every angry outburst I had, I was clearing the old pattern to make way for a more harmonious way of living.

Now, a year later, squabbles still arise, and I spend less time engaging with them. When I feel my temper rise, I take a walk or turn up the music and dance.

My teenager still complains and says, "You haven't changed a bit in four years."

That is his perception. I can feed it by getting angry and validating his statement or I can stay in my peace.

I am choosing peace and harmony most of the time now.

I am rewriting the story that parenting is tough. I am changing the story that someday later on I can start taking care of myself and pursue my dreams.

Instead, I am choosing to get right with myself by choosing to do things that I love even if my kids don't want to participate or join in.

Three years ago, just after my divorce, I continued to go to church even though my kids would never come with me. I would look around the congregation and see the nicely dressed families with Mom and Dad and Claire and Leo sitting attentively participating with interest in the service.

I asked the pastor one day after the service, "Pastor Doug, it is important to me to keep coming to church but I feel bad leaving my kids at home on Sunday morning. What can I do to encourage them to come?"

Pastor Doug said warmly, "Just keep coming. You are leading by example. Model the light and love of God. Eventually, some day, they may want to join you."

That hasn't happened yet. Even now with church services streamed online, my kids still won't sit around the computer in pajamas to attend worship with me.

The hardest thing for me to grasp these days is how to continue on the path with integrity when my own children (now teenagers) ridicule me. I must not take it personally, and I must trust that they, too, are still processing the upheaval of our family unit.

I thought the divorce would save our kids from the daily fights and disagreements. Magically, I thought our family would emerge happier and healthier and free from conflict.

We are headed that way, and I hold the vision of a healthy, harmonious home where everyone is safe, secure, supported, valued, and loved.

Soon, we will be moving from the home we lived in for nine years. We will leave behind memories and worn-out household items and start over in a new home.

I am changing the story, and I am ready for love to lead the way into a new home founded on respect, diligence, integrity, and teamwork.

A traditional Supermom measures her success by the success of her children. She does everything she can to ensure her kids will get into the best college and be on the most competitive sports team. There is scarcely a moment to breathe in her world because her days are packed with appointments, school functions, house chores, and work. Staying busy makes her feel important and needed. She rarely stops except for when her ill or fatigued body stops her in her tracks.

I am a woman who said NO! to the cult of moms putting their kids first. I am living life on my terms, and I am teaching my kids that it is okay to live their lives the way they see fit.

My son stopped attending classes in the middle of his sophomore year. He said most of the stuff they taught was outdated. For a gal who was a rule follower and perfectionist, I have had a challenging time embracing my son's renegade ways.

I love myself even when my son is flinging judgments at me. I still fly off the handle and stand up to defend myself. And then I remember, we are both works in progress.

When you decide to flip the switch on being what society calls a Supermom and instead become yourself, your kids will recognize your happiness. They might even want to be around you more.

You will spend months or even years flipping back between the roles of being a stereotypical Supermom and being yourself. With love and compassion, you will forgive yourself for doing too much, for living in the old worn-out story.

In time, the percentage of time you spend being your former Supermom self will be overshadowed by your vibrant, true, and healthy self. I am getting there but I still get stuck in comparison. You are redefining Supermom.

I think things like, *Why am I not further along in my business?*

And, *Why can't I have a kid who does community service and is captain of his team?*

Comparison always leads to judging myself unfairly.

I am enough. The more I love myself (all of me), the stronger I become. The stronger I become, the better I can handle the insults and blatant disrespect I experience from my children.

"Don't take things personally," I remind myself over and over.

You Are Enough

Do your best, Mom. Your best is good enough. You are enough as you are. No cape required.

Your superpower is being yourself with no compromises. In the end, being your true authentic self is one of the greatest gifts you can give your children.

When I began writing this book, the title was *I Am **Not** a Supermom*. Through my writing, I have come to discover that I am a Supermom after all. I used to criticize myself for my children's failures and for their disrespectful behavior. I now let my kids have their own experiences, and I can't wait to see how things unfold for each one, as I step away and lead by example. It has taken more strength to maintain my identity than to fall into the trap of mindlessly overburdening myself and my children with activities, events, and rules.

I feel secure in knowing that my kids are self-sufficient, free-thinking individuals who can create and find the experiences that are a good fit without directing, guiding, or forcing them into a box that they may discover later in life doesn't fit.

This Supermom has risen from the ashes of feeling responsible for making my kids happy to now making choices for myself. I have reclaimed my superpower and I am now thriving as a mother and a woman. And you can, too.

Endnotes

Chapter 2

[1] Pema Chodron, *When Things Fall Apart* (Boulder: Shambhala Publications, 2016).

[2] Dr. Shefali Tsabary, *The Awakened Family: A Revolution in Parenting* (New York: Viking Books, 2016).

[3] Pamela Starrett Ingalls, *Pressure Free Living* (Michigan: Self-Published, 2012).

Chapter 3

[1] Dr Wayne W Dyer, *Change Your Thoughts-Change Your Life* (Carlsbad: Hay House, 2009).

Chapter 4

[1] Parker, Kim, et al. "Survey of US Adults on Gender Differences: No Consensus on Nature versus Nurture." *Pew Research Center: Social and Demographic Trends*, 5 Dec. 2017.

Chapter 5

[1] "HopSkipDrive Releases Second Annual Survey on State of Back to School." *PRWeb*, 19 Sept. 2017, www.prweb.com/releases/2017/09/prweb14704772.htm.

About Gina

Gina realized she is a Supermom while writing this book. Having raised a child who fell short in terms of societal standards, Gina felt she had failed as a mother. However, through the process of writing, she discovered that how she handled herself through the challenges was evidence of her superpower to thrive in the face of adversity. She became a single mom of three kids after her divorce and learned to let go of her "mom-who-does-it-all" persona. Just as importantly, she learned to embrace the fact that she has many other marvelous facets in addition to being a mom. Daughter. Sister. Friend. Lover. Nature enthusiast. Peace seeker. Voracious learner. Lover of life.

As a personal trainer and women's wellness coach, Gina is a master of body mechanics and muscles. Her expertise in isolating muscles that are not functioning optimally allows her to reprogram their movements for healthy living. Dozens of women who have worked with her have claimed feeling more confident and at ease in their body, so they can enjoy exercise again. She specializes in pain relief and structural alignment and helps restore function and vigor to aging bodies. Gina encourages her training clients to move intuitively rather than force themselves to exercise; and once her clients gain Gina's tools and masterful approach to body awareness, they have the confidence to move in ways they never have before.

As a master of finding joy in movement, Gina believes the body is a playground to enjoy. Teaching yoga with live music and Tribal Beat, a meditative dance experience that she invented, unleashes her *inner hippie*. Her goal is to place a drum in the hands of as many women as possible, to show them the power of rhythm for stress relief and connecting with the heart. She loves camping near mountain streams and hiking amidst the summer wildflowers.

She's had a lifelong passion for tennis, spawned by her mother who took up tennis when she was pregnant with Gina. She aspires to be a top 10 USTA-ranked player in the "50 plus" category in Colorado. You will often find Gina walking her dogs in the park, throwing a baseball or football with her sons, or baking with her daughter. Above all else, Gina has learned to prioritize doing whatever makes her happy.

gina@ginafontaine.com

Instagram page @fontainegina

Acknowledgements

Thank you to my children Miles, Vienna and Ian who have courageously granted me permission to share our story so we, as a family, may help light the way for others who are struggling to find peace and harmony at home.

To Lynn, who edited my early drafts of this book and helped me create the vision of a book that would help millions of moms everywhere to know they are not alone in the struggle to keep up with the responsibilities of life. Thank you for encouraging me to keep writing even after I had shelved this project for months.

To Tal, you have given my family the opportunity to move from survival to thriving by generously opening your heart and home to us. Thank you for believing in me and giving me the security and support to see this project through to completion. Your honesty has illuminated my blind spots and broadened my vision.

To Pastor Laura who was a rock of truth and hope. You promised me that love and light always win and that my Easter Sunday would come. Thank you for seeing my light even when I was living in such darkness.

To the women of the Abiding Hope community who I first publicly shared my story with. Thank you for lovingly embracing me and hearing my message of loving yourself first with an open heart.

To the publishing and marketing team of Quantum Shift Media. Keren thank you for your creative vision and thought provoking writing prompts. After years of trying to figure out how I uniquely serve the world, you have finally helped solidify my unique message. Thank you for believing that this book can make a big impact on the world. To Stacy, thank you for managing the project and efficiently taking care of my requests. I feel confident that this project is in good hands with your excellent organization and listening skills.

To my coaches through the years-Victoria, Mike, David, Elle, Lila, Michelle, Katie, and Rachael Jayne - for guiding me on the path towards my truth and helping me turn weaknesses into strengths. Your wisdom and honesty have broken me open and helped me love and accept the fullness of who I am.

To Jennifer who masterfully captured my superpower in the photos that grace the cover of this book. To Cynthia, you have been with me through this entire journey. I never could have gotten through my divorce without our daily support calls. In my darkest moments, you were there to shine a light of hope that there could be something even better on the other side. Thank you for always asking me, "What would you rather have instead?"

To my friends and supporters - Paulette, Marta, Holly, Denise and Dan, Pierre and Donna, Miranda, Lori, Erin, the Peiffer family, Eunice, and all my clients who have stuck with me through the challenging times offering hope, support, prayers and advice.

To the court appointed support team and therapists who have supported my family through the worries, concerns and, at times, hopeless interactions. Thank you for seeing the potential in Miles and supporting all of us through these tumultuous times. My desperate phone calls and texts were never ignored and I appreciate your time, attention and unwavering support.

To my Mom, who demonstrated the importance of putting yourself first as a mother. You have endured the death of a son, supported three children through the horrors of mental illness and you continue to thrive as an octogenarian. You may have put off some of your own pursuits, like college, to be a mother, and ultimately you modeled for me how to be happy, vibrant and alive as a person who lives life fully and continually pursues learning new things.

To my Dad, you have always been there. I never felt like you judged me for my past mistakes. You loved me through all the bumps in the road and countless detours. Thank you for seeing me as the courageous, intelligent and successful woman that I am and believing that one day I would rise above the calamity. You once told me that "Worry is a slap in the face to God." Instead you have encouraged me to have fun and enjoy life even when the chips are down. Clearly those are words to live by as we celebrate your entry into the ninth decade of your life this year.

To all mothers, you inspire me with your relentless pursuit to find balance between work, family, social life, and household duties. Thank you for reading my story and being open to receive this message.

CPSIA information can be obtained
at www.ICGtesting.com
Printed in the USA
BVHW091342140921
616731BV00012B/230